IN SPIRIT AND IN TRUTH
—— A WORSHIP BOOK ——

EN ESPRIT ET EN VÉRITÉ
—— LOUANGES ET PRIERES ——

En Espíritu y en Verdad
—— LIBRO DE CULTO ——

IM GEIST UND IN DER WAHRHEIT
—— EIN GOTTESDIENSTBUCH ——

WORLD COUNCIL OF CHURCHES
SEVENTH ASSEMBLY 1991

CONSEIL OECUMENIQUE DES EGLISES
SEPTIEME ASSEMBLEE 1991

CONSEJO MUNDIAL DE IGLESIAS
SEPTIMA ASAMBLEA 1991

OKUMENISCHER RAT DER KIRCHEN
SIEBTE VOLLVERSAMMLUNG 1991

Cover: Illustration: "The Jesus Spirit in this Land", painting by Miriam Rose Ungunmerr, an Aboriginal artist. Photo: Rex Hunt.

Umschlag: Illustration: « Der Geist von Jesus in diesem Land », Malerei von Miriam Rose Ungunmerr, einer Aborigine-Künstlerin. Foto: Rex Hunt.

Couverture: Illustration: « L'esprit de Jésus sur notre terre », œuvre de Miriam Rose Ungunmerr, peintre aborigène. Photo: Rex Hunt.

Portada: Ilustración: « El Espíritu de Jesús en nuestra tierra », pintura de Miriam Rose Ungunmerr, artista aborigen. Fotografía: Rex Hunt.

Music typeset by Terry McArthur

Cover design by Edwin Hassink

ISBN 2-8254-0989-8

© 1991 World Council of Churches, 150 route de Ferney, 1211 Geneva 2, Switzerland

Printed in Australia by Pirie Printers

Published in collaboration with the Australian Council of Churches

JUDY JARVIS
MDEY
2 CHESTER HOUSE
PAGES LANE
LONDON N10 1PR

IN SPIRIT AND IN TRUTH
A WORSHIP BOOK

En Esprit et en Vérité
LOUANGES ET PRIERES

En Espíritu y en Verdad
LIBRO DE CULTO

IM GEIST UND IN DER WAHRHEIT
EIN GOTTESDIENSTBUCH

Contents

Inhaltsverzeichnis

Table des matières

Indice

Preface

When the day of Pentecost came, according to the Acts of the Apostles, the disciples were all together, gathered in one place. "And suddenly there was a sound from heaven like a violent wind blowing, and it filled the whole house where they were sitting. And they saw what looked like tongues of fire, coming to rest on every one of them. And they were all filled with the Holy Spirit, and began to talk in other tongues, as the Spirit enabled them to speak" (Acts 2:1-4). It was the fulfilment of what Christ had told his disciples. And it marked the beginning of the Church.

The disciples however did not reach Pentecost without preparation. They had first to retire to the upper room, and "pray with one mind, together with the women and Mary, the mother of Jesus, and his brothers" (Acts 1:14). It was by praying together that they prepared themselves to receive the Holy Spirit.

Our "upper room" in Canberra will be the worship tent. There thousands of people from all parts of the world, from East and West, from North and South, will together worship the Triune God. The tent will be the very centre of our life and work throughout the Assembly.

As we grapple with the issues we face, and struggle with all the items on the Assembly's agenda, our prayer will unceasingly go up to "God the Father, the original cause of all created things, the Son, the creative cause, and the Spirit, the perfecting cause", to use St Basil's famous words (*De Spiritu Sancto*, 38). Thus, the Assembly theme "Come, Holy Spirit — Renew the Whole Creation" will become a continuous invocation to the Holy Spirit, a waiting upon the Spirit, a prayer from the heart to perfect us and transform us into God's co-workers.

The worship book is designed to help us as we together wait upon the Spirit. It is a resource for our corporate acts of worship and celebration.

Our prayer is that the Holy Spirit, who is light and life and the source of all energy, may teach us how to pray, helping us in our weakness and interceding for us (Rom. 8:26).

Fr Georges Tsetsis
Moderator, Assembly Worship Committee

Vorwort

Als der Pfingsttag gekommen war, so heisst es in der Apostelgeschichte, waren die Jünger alle an einem Ort beieinander. «Und es geschah plötzlich ein Brausen vom Himmel wie von einem gewaltigen Wind und erfüllte das ganze Haus, in dem sie sassen. Und es erschienen ihnen Zungen, zerteilt wie von Feuer; und er setzte sich auf einen jeden von ihnen, und sie wurden alle erfüllt von dem heiligen Geist und fingen an, zu predigen in andern Sprachen, wie der Geist ihnen gab auszusprechen» (Apg 2, 1-4). So erfüllte sich, was Jesus seinen Jüngern gesagt hatte, und es war der Anfang der Kirche.

Die Ereignisse des Pfingsttages trafen die Jünger nicht unvorbereitet. Sie waren zunächst im Obergemach zusammengekommen, «einmütig im Gebet samt den Frauen und Maria, der Mutter Jesu, und seinen Brüdern» (Apg 1, 14). Im gemeinsamen Gebet bereiteten sie sich auf darauf vor, den Heiligen Geist zu empfangen.

Unser «Obergemach» in Canberra wird das Gottesdienstzelt sein. Tausende von Menschen aus allen Teilen der Welt, Ost und West, Nord und Süd, werden darin gemeinsam den dreieinigen Gott anbeten. Dieses Zelt wird der Mittelpunkt dessen sein, was wir auf der Vollversammlung erleben und erarbeiten.

Bei unserer Auseinandersetzung mit den Themen und Problembereichen und unserem Bemühen, alle Punkte auf der Tagesordnung der Vollversammlung zu behandeln, werden wir unaufhörlich zu «Gott, dem Vater», beten, «der die erste Ursache ist, zum Sohn, der die schaffende Ursache ist, und zum Heiligen Geist, der die vollendende Ursache ist», um mit dem Hl. Basilius zu sprechen (*De Spiritu Sancto*, 38). So wird das Thema der Vollversammlung zur unaufhörlichen Anrufung des Heiligen Geistes, zum Warten auf den Geist, zum Gebet aus ganzem Herzen darum, uns zu vervollkommnen und in Gottes Mitarbeiter und Mitarbeiterinnen zu verwandeln.

Das vorliegende Gottesdienstbuch soll uns eine Hilfe dabei sein, wenn wir gemeinsam auf den Geist warten. Es ist eine Quelle für unsere gemeinschaftlichen Gottesdienste und Feiern.

Wir beten darum, dass der Heilige Geist, der Licht und Leben und die Quelle aller Energie ist, uns beten lehre, dass er uns in unserer Schwachheit helfe und dass er für uns eintrete (Röm 8, 26).

Fr. Georges Tsetsis
Vorsitzender des Gottesdienstausschusses

Préface

Quand le jour de la Pentecôte arriva, lit-on dans les Actes des apôtres, les disciples se trouvaient réunis tous ensemble. «Tout à coup il y eut un bruit qui venait du ciel comme le souffle d'un violent coup de vent: la maison où ils se tenaient en fut toute remplie; alors leur apparurent comme des langues de feu qui se partageaient et il s'en posa sur chacun d'eux. Ils furent tous remplis d'Esprit Saint et se mirent à parler d'autres langues, comme l'Esprit leur donnait de s'exprimer» (Actes 2, 1-4). Ce jour-là s'accomplit ce que le

Christ avait annoncé à ses disciples. Ce fut aussi le jour qui marqua la naissance de l'Eglise.

Cependant, les disciples ne vécurent pas cet événement sans y avoir été d'abord préparés. Ils commencèrent par se retirer dans la chambre haute, où ils se mirent à prier : « Tous unanimes, étaient assidus à la prière, avec quelques femmes dont Marie la mère de Jésus, et avec les frères de Jésus » (Actes 1, 14). Ainsi, c'est par la prière qu'ils se préparèrent à recevoir l'Esprit Saint.

A Canberra, notre « chambre haute » sera la tente des cultes. C'est là que des milliers de gens venus de tous les coins du monde, du nord et du sud, de l'est et de l'ouest, célébreront ensemble le Dieu trinitaire. Ce lieu sera au cœur même de notre vie et de notre travail pendant toute la durée de l'Assemblée.

Tandis que nous nous attaquerons à la longue liste des points inscrits à notre ordre du jour et aux grandes questions qui nous interpellent aujourd'hui, notre prière ne cessera de s'élever. Elle s'élèvera — comme l'a dit saint Basile dans un texte célèbre — « vers le Père, la cause originelle ; vers le Fils, la cause créatrice ; vers l'Esprit, la cause parachevante de toutes les choses créées » (*De Spiritu Sancto*, 38). Ainsi, le thème de l'Assemblée « Viens, Esprit Saint, renouvelle toute la création » deviendra invocation incessante à l'Esprit Saint, attente de sa venue, prière du cœur, afin qu'Il nous conduise à la perfection et fasse de nous les collaborateurs de Dieu.

Ce recueil de louanges et prières nous accompagnera dans notre attente de la venue de l'Esprit. Il nous aidera à préparer ensemble nos actes communs de louange et de célébration.

Que l'Esprit Saint, qui est lumière et vie, et source de toute énergie, nous enseigne à prier en venant en aide à notre faiblesse et en intercédant pour nous (Rm 8, 26) !

Le Père Georges Tsetsis,
Président, Comité des cultes de l'Assemblée

Prefacio

Según los Hechos de los Apóstoles, cuando llegó el día de Pentecostés los discípulos estaban todos unánimes juntos. « Y de repente vino del cielo un estruendo como de un viento recio que soplaba, el cual llenó toda la casa donde estaban sentados; y se les aparecieron lenguas repartidas, como de fuego, asentándose sobre cada uno de ellos. Y fueron todos llenos del

Espíritu Santo, y comenzaron a hablar en otras lenguas según el Espíritu les daba que hablasen.» (Hechos 2: 1-4). Se había cumplido lo que Cristo había dicho a sus discípulos. Este hecho marcó el inicio de la Iglesia.

Sin embargo, los discípulos no habían llegado a Pentecostés sin previa preparación. Primero tuvieron que retirarse al aposento alto y «perseveraban unánimes en oración y ruego, con las mujeres, y con María la madre de Jesús, y con sus hermanos.» (Hechos 1:14). Se prepararon a recibir al Espíritu Santo orando juntos.

Nuestro «aposento alto» en Canberra será la carpa del culto. Allí, miles de personas de todas partes del mundo, de Oriente y Occidente, del Norte y del Sur, adorarán juntos al Dios Trino. La carpa será el verdadero centro de nuestra vida y labor a lo largo de la Asamblea.

A medida que intentemos resolver las cuestiones que se presentan y nos esforcemos en todos los puntos del orden del día de la Asamblea, nuestra oración se elevará incesantemente al «Dios Padre, la causa original de todas las cosas creadas, al Hijo, la causa creativa y al Espíritu, la causa consumadora», recurriendo a las famosas palabras de San Basilio (*De Spiritu Sancto*, 38). Así pues, el tema de la Asamblea, «Ven Espíritu Santo — Renueva toda la creación», se convertirá en una continua invocación al Espíritu Santo, una espera de la venida del Espíritu, una oración de todo corazón para que nos haga perfectos y nos transforme en colaboradores de Dios.

El propósito del libro de culto es ayudarnos mientras esperamos juntos la venida del Espíritu. Es una fuente para nuestros actos colectivos de culto y celebración.

Oremos para que el Espíritu Santo, que es luz y vida y fuente de toda la energía, nos enseñe a orar, nos ayude en nuestra debilidad e interceda por nosotros (Rom. 8:26).

Padre Georges Tsetsis
Moderador, Comité de Culto para la Asamblea

Introduction

"Come, Holy Spirit — Renew the Whole Creation" is the theme of the Seventh Assembly of the World Council of Churches which meets in Canberra, Australia, from 7 to 20 February 1991.

Some four thousand people from all parts of the world will assemble, and in the context of this invocatory prayer to the Spirit, will wait upon and seek the guidance of God's Spirit, as they review the work and witness of the WCC during the last eight years, and as they set the guidelines for its future work.

Prayer and worship are at the heart of an assembly — and the theme, which is itself a prayer, is a symbol of that. The study, the discussion and the debate happen within the context of worship. This book has been compiled to support such prayer and worship.

The book reflects the church in its ecumenical richness; it is both culturally and confessionally diverse. Whilst many prayers and songs are new, the richness of ancient traditions are also present. The compilers hope the book, together with the worship at the assembly, will expand liturgical horizons, and that the participants will share the hymns and worship forms of Christians from other cultures and traditions.

The first part of the book includes prayers on the theme of the Holy Spirit, in eight categories: invocations, calls to worship, praise and adorations, confessions, collects, affirmations of faith, intercessions and benedictions. Many of these prayers are repsonsive, and in these prayers the congregational part is printed in italics. In a few instances musical responses are printed with the prayers, but many more are available in the music section, and especially useful are the alleluias and kyries Nos 15-24. An index of prayers on page 191 relates the prayers to the assembly sub-themes.

The music section incorporates many short responses and songs which have been successful in ecumenical gatherings during and since the Vancouver Assembly. The move towards a more global representation of church music, and the sensitivity to indigenous culture, makes this a rich resource of church music. Where some effort is needed to learn tonalities or language sounds currently unfamiliar to the ecumenical family, the committee believes this will be rewarded many times over. So whilst simplicity is important, it is not the only criteria upon which music has been selected.

The worship of the Assembly will draw primarily from the resources within this book. The liturgies compiled for morning worship, plus the opening and closing worships will be available as a separate publication after the assembly. Page 1 offers the general outline for morning worship which will be used.

It is hoped that this book, inspired by the assembly theme, Come, Holy Spirit — Renew the Whole Creation, will enrich the worship life of God's people everywhere in the years to come. It is in this hope that the Assembly Worship Committee, and the WCC staff related to it, greet you in the name of Jesus Christ.

*   *   *

We are grateful to those who contributed material for the worship book. We acknowledge our thanks to individuals and organizations who have given us permission to use material already published. We also thank those who translated the prayers and songs.

Einführung

«Komm, Heiliger Geist — Erneuere die ganze Schöpfung» lautet das Thema der Siebten Vollversammlung des Ökumenischen Rates der Kirchen, die vom 7. bis 20. Februar 1991 in Canberra, Australien, stattfinden wird.

Rund viertausend Christen aus aller Welt werden sich dort versammeln; mit diesem Bittgebet zum Geist suchen und erwarten sie die Führung des Heiligen Geistes, wenn sie auf die Arbeit und das Zeugnis des ÖRK in den letzten acht Jahren zurückblicken und Richtlinien für die zukünftige Arbeit festlegen.

Gebet und Gottesdienst stehen im Mittelpunkt einer Vollversammlung — und das Thema, selbst ein Gebet, ist ein Symbol hierfür. Studienarbeit, Diskussion und Austausch vollziehen sich im Zusammenhang mit dem gottesdienstlichen Leben. Dieses Buch ist als Hilfestellung für Gebet und Gottesdienst zusammengestellt worden.

Dieses Gottesdienstbuch spiegelt den ökumenischen Reichtum der Kirche wider und bietet eine kulturelle und konfessionelle Vielfalt. Während viele Gebete und Lieder neu sind, zeigt das Buch auch den Reichtum der alten Traditionen auf. Die für die Zusammenstellung Verantwortlichen hoffen, dass das vorliegende Buch — zusammen mit der Gotterdiensterfahrung auf der Vollversammmlung — unsere liturgischen Horizonte erweitern wird und dass die Teilnehmer und Teilnehmerinnen angeregt werden, die Lieder und Gottesdienstformen von Christen aus anderen Kulturen und Traditionen in die eigene aufzunehmen.

Der erste Teil des Buches schliesst Gebete zum Thema des Heiligen Geistes in acht Kategorien ein: Anrufungen, Aufruf zum Gottesdienst, Lobpreis und Anbetung, Bekenntnis, Kollektengebete, Glaubensbekenntnisse, Fürbittgebete und Segen. Viele dieser Gebete sind Wechselgesänge, in diesen ist die Antwort der Gemeinde kursiv gedruckt. An einigen Stellen sind Wechselgesänge zusammen mit den Gebeten abgedruckt, aber viele weitere sind in dem musikalischen Teil enthalten; besonders hilfreich sind das Halleluja und die Kyrie-Gesänge (Nr. 15-24). Ein Verzeichnis der Gebete auf S. 191 stellt den Bezug der Gebete zu den Unterthemen der Vollversammlung her.

Der musikalische Teil schliesst viele kurze Wechselgesänge und Lieder ein, die auf ökumenischen Zusammenkünften während und seit Vancouver viel

Anklang gefunden haben. Die Bewegung auf eine umfassendere Vorstellung der kirchlichen Musik und auf das Feingefühl für einheimische Kulturen macht diesen Teil zu einer reichen Quelle der kirchlichen Musik. Der Gottesdienstausschuss ist der Überzeugung, dass die Anstrengungen, Tonalitäten oder Sprachtöne zu erlernen, die der ökumenischen Familie noch unbekannt sind, vielfach belohnt werden. Während also Einfachheit ein wichtiges Merkmal ist, darf sie nicht als das einzige Merkmal gelten, aufgrund dessen die Musik ausgesucht wird.

Die Andachten und Gottesdienste auf der Vollversammlung werden in erster Linie aus dem Vorrat dieses Buches schöpfen. Die Liturgien, die für die Morgenandachten zusammengestellt worden sind sowie die Ordnungen des Eröffnungs- und Abschlussgottesdienstes werden nach der Vollversammlung als eine gesonderte Veröffentlichung erhältlich sein. Auf S. 31 finden Sie einen allgemeinen Aufriss für die täglichen Morgengottesdienste.

Es bleibt zu hoffen, dass dieses Gottesdienstbuch — angeregt durch das Thema der Vollversammlung «Komm, Heiliger Geist — erneuere die ganze Schöpfung» das gottesdienstliche Leben des Volkes Gottes in den kommenden Jahren überall auf der Welt bereichern wird. In dieser Hoffnung grüssen Sie der Gottesdienstausschuss für die Vollversammlung und der mit ihm zusammenarbeitende Mitarbeiterstab des ÖRK im Namen Jesu Christi.

* * *

Wir danken all denen, die Material für dieses Gottesdienstbuch beigetragen haben. Ferner möchten wir allen Einzelpersonen und Organisationen danken, die uns den Nachdruck bereits veröffentlichter Materialien gestattet haben. Wir danken ebenfalls allen, die uns bei der Übersetzung der Gebete und Lieder geholfen haben.

Introduction

« Viens, Esprit Saint, renouvelle toute la création », est le thème de la Septième Assemblée du Conseil œcuménique des Eglises qui se réunit à Canberra, en Australie, du 7 au 20 février 1991.

Quatre mille chrétiens venus du monde entier se rassembleront et, portés par cette prière d'invocation à l'Esprit, s'attendront à sa présence et à son inspiration, tandis qu'ils passeront en revue le témoignage et les activités du COE durant les huit années passées et qu'ils définiront les grandes orientations de ses activités futures.

La prière et l'esprit d'adoration sont au cœur d'un tel rassemblement : le thème choisi en est le symbole. La réflexion, les échanges et les débats s'insèrent dans un contexte de prière et de recueillement — personnel et collectif — et c'est pour y contribuer que ce recueil est publié.

L'ouvrage que voici est à l'image de l'Eglise dans toute sa richesse œcuménique, un reflet de sa diversité culturelle et confessionnelle. Si de nombreuses prières et textes chantés sont nouveaux, la richesse des anciennes traditions a été conservée. L'équipe de rédaction espère que ce recueil, ainsi que les célébrations durant l'Assemblée, permettront à chacun d'élargir son horizon liturgique et que tous les participants auront plaisir à découvrir des cantiques ou des formes liturgiques utilisés par des chrétiens d'autres traditions culturelles.

La première partie du présent ouvrage comprend des prières sur le thème du Saint Esprit, sous huit rubriques différentes : invocation, invitation à la prière, louange et adoration, confession des péchés, recueillement, affirmation de la foi, intercession et bénédiction. Un certain nombre de prières prévoient des répons dits par l'ensemble des participants : ils sont imprimés en italiques. La musique accompagne certains textes, mais d'autres mélodies se trouvent dans la partie musicale : en particulier des « alléluias » et des « kyrie », aux Nos 15-24. Un répertoire en page 191 fait correspondre les titres des rubriques aux sous-thèmes de l'assemblée.

La section musicale réunit bon nombre de chants et de répons très prisés lors de l'assemblée de Vancouver et qui furent souvent utilisés ces dernières années dans d'autres rencontres. Le soin pris à inclure un éventail toujours plus large de musique religieuse et à veiller au respect des cultures locales devrait faire de cette partie musicale un auxiliaire utile de l'activité musicale des Eglises. La peine qu'on aura prise pour se familiariser avec des tonalités ou des sonorités linguistiques peu connues de la famille œcuménique — le comité en est persuadé — se verra également récompensée dans le cours du temps. Dès lors que la simplicité reste le premier critère, il n'est pas le seul.

Les célébrations et les prières de l'assemblée s'inspireront d'abord des éléments contenus dans ce recueil. Les schémas des recueillements matinaux, ainsi que ceux des cultes d'ouverture et de clôture, seront publiés à part, à l'issue de l'Assemblée. Page 61 propose un canevas qui sera utilisé lors des recueillements du matin.

Puisse le présent recueil — rédigé en s'inspirant du thème choisi pour l'Assemblée, « Viens, Esprit Saint, renouvelle toute la création » — contribuer à l'enrichissement de la vie cultuelle et liturgique du peuple de Dieu, où qu'il soit, dans le courant des années à venir.

* * *

Notre reconnaissance s'adresse à tous ceux qui ont fourni des documents
utilisés dans ce recueil : en particulier aux personnes et aux organisations
dont les contributions sont déjà publiées ailleurs. Nous remercions également
les traducteurs de diverses prières et cantiques.

Introducción

« Ven Espíritu Santo — Renueva toda la Creación » es el tema de la Séptima
Asamblea del Consejo Mundial de Iglesias que se reunirá en Canberra,
Australia, desde el 7 al 20 de febrero de 1991.

Se congregarán unas cuatro mil personas de todas partes del mundo, y en el
marco de esta invocación al Espíritu, esperarán y buscarán la guía del
espíritu de Dios al examinar la labor y el testimonio del CMI durante los
últimos ocho años, y establecerán las directrices para su trabajo futuro.

La oración y la adoración son partes centrales del programa de la Asamblea
— y el tema, que es en sí una oración, es un símbolo de ello. La labor de
estudio, la discusión y los debates se realizan dentro del marco del culto.
Este libro ha sido realizado para sustentar dicha oración y adoración.

El libro refleja la riqueza ecuménica de la iglesia, y presenta una gran
diversidad cultural y confesional. Mientras muchas oraciones y canciones
son nuevas, también está presente la riqueza de las antiguas tradiciones. Sus
autores esperan que este libro, junto al culto durante la Asamblea, contribuya
a extender los horizontes litúrgicos, y que las personas que lo utilicen
compartan cánticos y formas cúlticas de cristianos que viven en otras culturas
y tradiciones.

La primera parte del libro contiene oraciones acerca del tema del Espíritu
Santo, en ocho subtemas : invocaciones, llamados a la adoración, alabanzas
y adoración, confesiones, colectas, afirmaciones de fe, intercesiones y
bendiciones. Muchas de estas oraciones son antifonales y en ellas la
respuesta congregacional está impresa en bastardilla. En algunos casos las
respuestas musicales están impresas con las oraciones, pero la mayoría se
encuentran en la sección del himnario, y son especialmente útiles los
aleluyas y kyries Nos. 15-24. El índice de oraciones en la página 191 las
relaciona con los subtemas de la asamblea.

La sección musical incorpora muchas respuestas breves y canciones que han
sido muy populares en reuniones ecuménicas durante y desde la Asamblea de

Vancouver. El intento de lograr una representación más global de la música eclesiástica, y la sensibilidad a la cultura indígena, hace de éste un rico recurso de música eclesiástica. El comité cree que los esfuerzos realizados para aprender tonalidades o sonidos lingüísticos usualmente desconocidos para la familia ecuménica serán ampliamente recompensados. Así, mientras la simplicidad es lo importante, no es el único criterio sobre el cual se seleccionó la música.

El culto en la Asamblea se basará principalmente en los recursos contenidos en este libro. Las liturgias recopiladas para los cultos matutinos, más los cultos de apertura y de clausura estarán disponibles en publicaciones separadas después de la Asamblea. La página 91 ofrece una guía general para los cultos matutinos.

Cabe esperar que este libro, inspirado en el tema de la Asamblea — «Ven Espíritu Santo — Renueva toda la Creación», pueda enriquecer la vida cúltica del pueblo de Dios en el mundo entero durante los próximos años. Con esta esperanza, el Comité de Culto para la Asamblea y el personal del CMI que colabora con dicho Comité, los saluda en el nombre de Jesucristo.

* * *

Deseamos expresar nuestro agradecimiento a todos los que han aportado material para el libro de culto, así como a las personas y organizaciones que nos han autorizado a utilizar textos ya publicados. Agradecemos también a quienes tradujeron las oraciones y canciones.

Order for daily worship

Preparation
Invocation
Psalm or Hymn of praise
Confession of sins, word of forgiveness

Entry of the Word
Old Testament or Epistle reading
Gospel reading
Acclamation
Response to the Word

Affirmation of faith
Intercessions
Lord's Prayer

Benediction

Hymn

I. Invocations

1
God of grace and holiness,
send upon us today your Holy Spirit
as you sent the Spirit upon the apostles
on the day of Pentecost,
so that our prayers and our deeds
may bear witness to this desire which possesses us:
We wish to be one, Lord,
so that the world may believe that we belong to you.
Fill us now with your love.

2
O Light!
Divine and one Holy Trinity,
we, born of the earth,
glorify you always
together with the heavenly hosts.
At the raising of the morning light
shine forth upon our souls
your intelligible light.

3
Flame of the Spirit:
warm our hearts to love our neighbour.

Flame of the Spirit:
light our path that we may walk in truth.

Flame of the Spirit:
rise in us with a passion for freedom.

Flame of the Spirit:
gather us together in the celebration of your life.

4
O Heavenly King, Comforter, Spirit of truth,
present in all places and filling all things;
treasury of blessings and giver of life:
Come and dwell in us, cleanse us from every impurity,
and of your goodness save our souls.

5   O God, the Holy Spirit,
         come to us, and among us:
         come as the wind, and cleanse us;
         come as the fire, and burn;
         come as the dew, and refresh;
         convict, convert, and consecrate
         many hearts and lives
         to our great good
         and thy greater glory,
         and this we ask for Jesus Christ's sake.

6   Come, Holy Spirit,
         Inflame our waiting hearts!

         Burn us with your love,
         Renew us in your life.

7   Spirit of light: let your wisdom shine on us.
         Spirit of God, come into our hearts, make us your new creation.

         Spirit of silence: make us aware of God's presence.
         (Response as above)

         Spirit of courage: dispel the fear in our hearts.
         (Response as above)

         Spirit of fire: inflame us with Christ's love.
         (Response as above)

         Spirit of peace: help us be still and listen to God's Word.
         (Response as above)

         Spirit of joy: inspire us to proclaim the good news.
         (Response as above)

         Spirit of love: help us to open ourselves to the needs of others.
         (Response as above)

         Spirit of power: give us all your help and strength.
         (Response as above)

         Spirit of truth: guide us all in the way of Christ.
         (Response as above)

8   Sisters and brothers — Arise.
Arise and lift your hearts
Arise and lift your eyes
Arise and lift your voices.

The living God,
the living, moving Spirit of God
has called us together —
in witness
in celebration
in struggle.

Reach out towards each other.
for our God reaches out towards us!
Let us worship God!

9   Let the heavens rejoice, and let the earth be glad.
Let the sea roar and all that fills it;
Let the fields exult, and everything in it.
Then shall the trees of the wood
sing for joy before the Lord,
For he comes to judge the world with righteousness
and the peoples with his truth.

(silence)

The work of God surrounds us,
we respond with praise.

The love of God is visible,
we respond in faith.

The word of God is calling,
we respond in hope.

The wind of the Spirit is blowing,
we respond with joy.

10   Pray for the raising of river waters this year,
that Christ, our Lord,
may bless it and raise it to its measure,
grant a cheerful touch
unto the lands,
support the human beings,
save the cattle
and forgive us our sins.
Lord, have mercy.

Pray for the trees, vegetations
and land plantations this year,
that Christ, our Lord, may bless them
to grow and bring forth
plentiful fruit, have compassion upon his creation
and forgive us our sins.
Lord, have mercy.

Accord, O Lord, a cheerful touch unto the earth,
water it,
and dispose our life as deemed fit.
Crown this year with your goodness,
for the sake of the poor of your people,
the widow, the orphan, the stranger
and for our sake.
For our eyes are focussed upon you, our hope,
and seek your holy name.
You provide us our food in due course.
Deal with us, O Lord, according to your goodness,
you, the feeder of everybody.
Fill our hearts with joy and grace,
that, as we always have sufficiently of all things,
we grow in every good deed.
Amen.

II. Calls to worship

11   The world belongs to God,
the earth and all its people.

How good and how lovely it is
to live together in unity.

Love and faith come together,
justice and peace join hands.

If the Lord's disciples keep silent
these stones would shout aloud.

Lord, open our lips
and our mouths shall proclaim your praise.

12   Rejoice, people of God!
Celebrate the life within you,
and Christ's presence in your midst!

Our eyes shall be opened!
The present will have new meaning,
and the future will be bright with hope.

Rejoice, people of God!
Bow your heads before the One
who is our wisdom and our strength.

We place ourselves before our God,
that we may be touched and cleansed
by the power of God's spirit.

13   In mystery and grandeur
we see the face of God
in earthiness and the ordinary
we know the love of Christ.

In heights and depths
and life and death:
the spirit of God
is moving among us.

Let us praise God.

14   I will light a light
        in the name of God
        who lit the world
        and breathed the breath of life into me.

        I will light a light
        in the name of the Son
        who saved the world
        and stretched out his hand to me.

        I will light a light
        in the name of the Spirit
        who encompasses the world
        and blesses my soul with yearning.

        We will light three lights
        for the trinity of love:

        God above us,
        God beside us,
        God beneath us:
        the beginning,
        the end,
        the everlasting one.

15   Sisters and brothers
        we have come together
        to worship God who offers us freedom
        through our Lord Jesus Christ.
        For the spirit of life in Christ Jesus
        has set us free from the law of sin and death.
        For we did not receive the spirit of slavery
        to fall back into fear
        but we have received the spirit
        of the children of God.

16   We reverently worship
        the mysterious Person, God the Father,
        the responding Person, God the Son,
        the witnessing Person, the Spirit of Holiness.
        We worship the Holy Trinity
        Three persons in one.

III. Praise and adoration

17 Jesus, as a mother you gather your people to you:
You are gentle with us as a mother with her children.

Often you weep over our sins and our pride:
Tenderly you draw us from hatred and judgement.

You comfort us in sorrow and bind up our wounds:
In sickness you nurse us, and with pure milk you feed us.

Jesus, by your dying we are born to new life:
By your anguish and labour we come forth in joy.

Despair turns to hope through your sweet goodness:
Through your gentleness we find comfort in fear.

Your warmth gives life to the dead:
Your touch makes sinners righteous.

Lord Jesus, in your mercy heal us:
In your love and tenderness remake us.

In your compassion bring grace and forgiveness:
For the beauty of heaven may your love prepare us.

A Song of St Anselm

18 From before the world began
and after the end of eternity,
you are God.

From the sea bursting out of its womb
to the wind ceasing from its chase,
you are God.

In the constancy of created things
and in their fickleness,
you are God.

In the vastness of the universe
and the forgotten corner of our hearts,
you are God.
You are our God,
and we bless you.

19   Glory to you, Almighty God!
You spoke, and light came out of darkness,
order rose from confusion.

(Women:)
You breathed into the dust of the earth,
and we were formed in your image.

(Men:)
You looked on the work of your hands,
and declared that it was all good.

And still you speak, breathe and look for us.
We praise you!

Glory to you, Jesus Christ!
You met us as a refugee, a threatened child,
the word made flesh, born in a forgotten place.

(Women:)
You called us, by name, to leave what was comfortable,
to be your disciples, companions and friends.

(Men:)
You saved us by kneeling at our feet,
stretching your arms wide to take away our sins,
walking through death to life again.

And still you meet, call and save us.
We praise you!

Glory to you, Holy Spirit!
You brooded over chaos,
mothering and shaping God's new creation.

(Women:)
You inspired prophets and evangelists
to discover the right word for the right season.

(Men:)
You liberated the early church for mission,
claiming all of life for the Lord of all.

And still you brood over, inspire and liberate us.
We praise you!

Glory to you, God, Three-in-One!
You are surrounded by the song of the saints in heaven,
and you are present with us now.
We adore you!

20

I saw water flowing from the threshold of the temple:
where the river flows everything will spring to life.

On the banks of the river grow trees bearing
every kind of fruit:
their leaves will not wither nor their fruit fail.

Their fruit will serve for food,
their leaves for the healing of the nations:
for the river of the water of life
flows from the throne of God and of the lamb.

IV. Confessions

21

Lord, your ways are not our ways:
your thoughts are not our thoughts:
what to us seems like eternity
is only a moment to you.

In the face of eternity,
help us to be humble.

Traditional Urdu   R.F. Liberius: Pakistan

1. Khu-da - ya,   ra - hem kar.   Khu - da - ya,   ra - hem,
   Have mer - cy   on us, Lord,   have mer - cy   on us.

Khu-da - ya,   ra - hem kar. Khu - da - ya,   ra - hem.
Have mer - cy   on us, Lord, have mer - cy   on us.

Khu— da - ya, ra - hem kar, khu - da - ya, ra - hem.
Have mer - cy on us, Lord, have mer - cy on us.

Kyrie eleison. Herr, erbarme dich. Seigneur, aie pitié de nous. Señor, ten piedad de nosotros.
Christe eleison. Christe, erbarme dich. O Christ, aie pitié de nous. Christo, ten piedad de nosotros.

If we have been singing praises with our voices
and kept the joy out of our hearts;

If we have prayed only for what was possible
and hoped only for what we could see;

If we have taken your grace for granted
and expected instant answers to immediate requests;

If we have allowed waiting on your Spirit to slip into laziness
and waiting on the Kingdom to be replaced by apathy;

If we have only thought of us waiting on you
and never pondered how you wait on us:

2. Ma— si - ha, ra - hem kar, ma - si - ha, ra - hem.
Have mer - cy on us, Christ, have mer - cy on us.

Ma— si - ha, ra - hem kar, ma - si - ha, ra hem.
Have mer - cy on us, Christ, have mer - cy on us.

Ma— si - ha, ra - hem kar, ma - si - ha, ra - hem.
Have mer - cy on us, Christ, have mer - cy on us.

Kyrie eleison. Herr, erbarme dich. Seigneur, aie pitié de nous. Señor, ten piedad de nosotros.
Christe eleison. Christe, erbarme dich. O Christ, aie pitié de nous. Christo, ten piedad de nosotros.

If we have prayed, "Giver of Life, Sustain your Creation"
and succumbed to the economics of consumption.

If we have prayed, "Spirit of Truth, Set us Free"
and chosen instead the slavery of silence.

If we have prayed, "Spirit of Unity, Reconcile your people"
and have not met with persons of other confessions or traditions in our own
neighbourhood.

If we have prayed, "Holy Spirit, Transform and Sanctify us"
and not expected the Spirit to change our lives:

Traditional Urdu   R.F. Liberius: Pakistan

3. Khu- da - ya,   ra - hem kar.   Khu- da - ya,   ra - hem,
   Have mer - cy   on us, Lord,   have mer - cy   on us.

Khu- da - ya,   ra - hem kar. Khu - da - ya,   ra - hem.
Have mer - cy   on us, Lord, have mer - cy   on us.

Khu — da - ya, ra - hem   kar,   khu - da - ya, ra - hem.
Have   mer - cy on   us, Lord,   have mer - cy on us.

Kyrie eleison. Herr, erbarme dich. Seigneur, aie pitié de nous. Señor, ten piedad de nosotros.
Christe eleison. Christe, erbarme dich. O Christ, aie pitié de nous. Christo, ten piedad de nosotros.

Listen, for this is the true word of God
blessed are all who wait for the Lord
God is merciful, and God's love is sure and strong.
Amen.

22   Spirit of joy,
        through you, Christ lives in us,
        and we in Christ.
        Forgive us when we forget you
        and when we fail to live in your joy.
        Spirit of God, forgive us,
        and lead us to life in you.

        Spirit of love,
        you bind us in love to yourself
        and to those around us,
        in marriage, in family and in friendship.
        Forgive us when we hurt those we love
        and when we turn away from the love of our friends.
        Spirit of God, forgive us,
        and lead us to life in you.

        Spirit of the Body of Christ,
        uniting us in the church
        with your life-giving grace and hope.
        Forgive our fragmenting of your church
        and our failure to carry your love into the world.
        Spirit of God, forgive us,
        and lead us to life in you.

        Spirit in the world,
        comforting us, and drawing us into closer
        relationship with one another.
        Forgive our wars and our hatreds,
        and forgive our failure to recognize you,
        who lives in us all.
        Spirit of God, forgive us,
        and lead us to life in you.

        As the dove gently settles on the tree,
        receive the gift of peace.
        As the flame rises free with light and warmth,
        receive the gift of life.
        As the wind moves and dances round the earth,
        receive the gracious gift of the Spirit.
        Amen.

23   Lord Jesus Christ,
        Son of the living God,
        have mercy on me,
        a sinner.

24 You have called us out of death,
we praise you!
Send us back with the bread of life,
we pray you!

You have caused us to turn around
we praise you!
Keep us ever faithful to you,
we pray you!

You have begun the work of grace,
we praise you!
Complete your salvation in us,
we pray you!

You have made us your people,
we praise you!
Make us one with all people
We pray you!

25 In faith
let us come before the Holy God
and know who we are:
(silent prayer)

We are the people of the New Heaven
and the New Earth,
but we fall far short of that hope.

We are the people who receive
the grace of God,
but we fail to offer it to others.

Ask and you shall receive,
seek and you shall find,
knock and life will be
opened before you.
Rise up and live
in freedom and faith.
Amen.

26   Holy Spirit, Advocate and Comforter,
In you we celebrate the liberating presence of the living Christ.
You blow where you will, refreshing, renewing and inspiring;
Like fire you purify.

Holy Spirit, Advocate and Comforter,
You expose what is evil in the world.
You convict the world of sin;
Like fire you purify.

Purify us, carry us beyond our narrow personal concerns;
Uphold, preserve and care for your creation,
Nourish, sustain and direct your creatures.
Holy Spirit, Advocate and Comforter,
Like fire you purify.
Purify us, we pray.

27   Let us confess
the secret sins in the hidden spaces of our lives,
which hold us in fear and anguish,
keeping us from God and from each other.

(silence)

Korean   Jacques Berthier: Taizé France

Chu-yo   chu - yo   tu-ro   chu-so-so.   Chu-yo   chu— yo   tu-ro   chu-so-so.

Lord hear us. Höre uns, Gott. Ecoute nous, Dieu. Seigneur, aie pitié. Señor, escúchanos.

Let us confess
the words of judgement we have withheld in our societies,
the compromises we have made which allow evil to multiply,
producing harvests of destruction and death.

(silence)

Korean   Jacques Berthier: Taizé France

Chu-yo   chu - yo   tu - ro   chu-so-so.   Chu-yo   chu— yo   tu - ro   chu-so-so.

Lord hear us. Höre uns, Gott. Ecoute nous, Dieu. Seigneur, aie pitié. Señor, escúchanos.

Let us confess
the complacency with which we live in disunity,
the ease with which we keep our prejudices,
refusing to be the one people of God for which Jesus prayed.

(silence)

Response

God from whom nothing is hidden
and who knows the motives of our hearts,
forgives us our sins
and declares to us the joyful truth
that we are a liberated people.

V. Collects

28   Spirit of truth and judgement,
        who alone can exorcize
        the powers that grip our world,
        at the point of crisis
        give us your discernment,
        that we may accurately name what is evil,
        and know the way that leads to peace,
        through Jesus Christ,
        Amen.

29   O God our disturber,
        whose speech is pregnant with power
        and whose word will be fulfilled,
        may we know ourselves unsatisfied
        with all that distorts your truth,

1.
Baptism of Christ / Taufe Christi
Baptême du Christi / El Bautismo de Cristo

2.
Pentecost / Pfingsten
Pentecôte / Pentecostés

and make our hearts attentive
to your liberating voice,
in Jesus Christ,
Amen.

30   Almighty God, your word of creation
caused the water to be filled
with many kinds of living beings
and the air to be filled with birds.
With those who live in this world's small islands
we rejoice in the richness of your creation,
and we pray for your wisdom
for all who live on this earth,
that we may wisely manage and not destroy what you have made
for us and for our descendants.
In Jesus' name we pray.
Amen.

31   O God, our Creator,
who gave us all
that we are and have:
release us from self-love
to be able to share
what we are
what we know
what we have
with one another
[in this Assembly] and in the world which you love.
In the name of Christ
who makes this sharing possible.
Amen.

32   Spirit of energy and change,
in whose power Jesus was anointed
to be the hope of the nations;
be poured out also upon us
without reserve or distinction,
that we may have confidence and strength
to plant your justice on the earth,
through Jesus Christ.
Amen.

VI. Creeds

33
We believe in one God,
the Father, the Almighty,
maker of heaven and earth,
of all that is, seen and unseen.

We believe in one Lord, Jesus Christ,
the only Son of God,
eternally begotten of the Father,
Light from Light,
true God from true God,
begotten, not made,
of one Being with the Father:
through him all things were made.
For us and for our salvation he came down from heaven;
by the power of the Holy Spirit he became incarnate
from the Virgin Mary
and was made man.
For our sake he was crucified under Pontius Pilate;
he suffered death and was buried;
on the third day he rose again in accordance with the scriptures;
he ascended into heaven.

He is seated at the right hand of the Father,
he will come again in glory
to judge the living and the dead,
and his kingdom will have no end.

We believe in the Holy Spirit,
the Lord, the giver of life,
who proceeds from the Father;
with the Father and the Son
he is worshipped and glorified;
he has spoken through the Prophets.
We believe in one, holy, catholic and apostolic Church.
We acknowledge one baptism for the forgiveness of sins.
We look for the resurrection of the dead,
and the life of the world to come.
Amen.

Nicene-Constantinopolitan Creed

34 I believe in God,
    the Father almighty,
    Creator of heaven and earth.

    I believe in Jesus Christ,
    his only Son, our Lord.
    He was conceived
    by the power of the Holy Spirit,
    and born of the Virgin Mary.
    He suffered under Pontius Pilate,
    was crucified, died,
    and was buried.
    He descended to the dead.
    On the third day
    he rose again.
    He ascended into heaven,
    and is seated
    at the right hand of the Father.
    He will come again
    to judge the living and the dead.

    I believe in the Holy Spirit,
    the holy, catholic Church,
    the communion of saints,
    the forgiveness of sins,
    the resurrection of the body,
    and the life everlasting.
    Amen.

                    Apostles' Creed

VII. Intercessions

35 O God our Father,
    save our shores from the weapons of death,
    our lands from what may deny our young ones love and freedom.
    Let the seas [of the Pacific Ocean]
    carry messages of peace and goodwill.
    Turn away from our midst any unkind and brutal practices.
    Let our children swim, and breathe the fresh air
    that is filled by the Holy Spirit.

O Lord Jesus,
bless all who are makers of that inner peace
which breaks down the barriers of hatred;
and unite us with the open arms of your cross,
that all the peoples of the world may live happily together.
Amen.

36　　　O God,
You are the giver of life.
We pray for the Church in the whole world.
Sanctify her life, renew her worship,
give power to her witnessing,
restore her unity.
Give strength to those who are searching together
for that kind of obedience which creates unity.
Heal the divisions separating your children one
from another,
so that they will make fast, with bonds of peace,
the unity which the Spirit gives.
Amen.

37　　　O God,
you love justice and you establish peace on earth.
We bring before you the disunity of today's world:
the absurd violence, and the many wars, which are
breaking the courage of the peoples of the world;
militarism and the armaments race, which are
threatening life on the planet;
human greed and injustice, which breed hatred and strife.
Send your spirit and renew the face of the earth:
teach us to be compassionate toward the whole human family;
strengthen the will of all those who fight for justice
and for peace; lead all nations into the path of peace,
and give us that peace which the world cannot give.
Amen.

38　　　Lord, through the shedding of the blood of your martyrs,
gather in joy all the scattered children of your church,
and all who weep bitterly at the sadness of disunity,
you who give grace for our salvation.

39   Let us ask God for the coming of the kingdom.

           O God, into the pain of the tortured:
           breathe stillness.

           Into the hunger of the very poor:
           breathe fullness.

           Into the wounds of our planet:
           breathe well-being.

           Into the deaths of your creatures:
           breathe life.

           Into those who long for you:
           breathe yourself.

           Your kingdom come,
           your will be done.
           The kingdom, the power and the glory
           are yours now and forever.

           Our God is with us.

           We celebrate the miracle of living and being!
           We celebrate the miracle of Creation!
           Our God loves us,
           our lives are the blessing of God,
           let us give thanks with joy!
           Amen.

40   As we share the life of your church today,
           we pray that our witness will be true to Christ.
           Give us a voice for the silenced.
           And quiet communion,
           when only silence will honour pain.

           Give us tears in the face of grief.
           And laughter as we experience the joys of your creation.

           Give us sharpness in the revealing of injustice.
           And your eternal gentleness with those
           who cross our path in despair.

Give us integrity in admitting our confusions.
And faithfulness in our life with our neighbours.
For you call us to work with you in confident relationship, believing
that our prayers are the joining of our love, with your love,
for the world.

In the grace of God lies the infinite possibility of hope.
Amen.

41

Remember, Lord, the down-coming of the rains and the waters and the rivers, and bless them.

Remember, Lord, the plants and the seeds and the fruits of the fields of every year, bless them and make them abundant.

Remember, Lord, the safety of your own holy church and all the cities and countries.

Remember, Lord, the safety of humankind and of beasts and of me, your sinful servant.

Remember, Lord, our fathers and mothers, our brothers and sisters who have fallen asleep and gone to their rest.

Remember, Lord, the captives of your people, and bring them again in peace to their dwelling place.

Remember, Lord, the afflicted and distressed.

Remember, Lord, your servants, the poor who are under oppression, have pity upon them and keep them in the right faith and make them a dwelling place of the Holy Spirit, through our spiritual joy and the love of humankind.
Amen.

42

O God, be present among us, for the sake of all human beings on earth.
Open our eyes that we may see the salvation which is in you, and reveal yourself to a blind humanity.

Make your face shine upon those stricken with disease.
Give them your strength and your peace.

All the poor ones, the weak, all those weighed down by want, may they have the knowledge of you, so to lean on you and be filled to overflowing in you.

To the mighty and the wealthy, grant the power they are lacking.
Give them a discerning spirit, that they may be free by your freedom, and
free to love others.

To one and all of us, may you grant your life and your peace.
Amen.

43   Where ignorance, self-love and insensitivity
        have fractured life in community,
        give your light, O God of love.

        Where injustice and oppression have broken
        the spirit of peoples,
        give your light, O God who frees.

        Where hunger and poverty, illness and death
        have made life an unbearable burden,
        give your light, O God of grace.

        Where suspicion and hatred, conflict and war
        have challenged your goodness,
        give your light, O God of peace.

        Eternal God,
        open the eyes of the nations and peoples
        so that they may walk in the light of love;
        remove the ignorance and stubbornness of nations and peoples
        so that they may drink from the fountains of your goodness.
        Amen.

44   Come, Holy Spirit, renew the whole creation.
        Send the wind and flame
        of your transforming life
        to lift up the church in this day.
        Give wisdom and faith
        that we may know
        the great hope to which we are called.
        Come Holy Spirit,
        renew the whole creation.

Giver of life,
sustain your creation.
Confront us with
our greedy consuming of your gifts.
Stand before us
as we pillage and destroy.
Call us forth
into new harmonies of care
for all that lives and breathes
and has its being.
Come, Holy Spirit,
renew the whole creation.

Spirit of truth,
set us free
to emerge as the children of God.
Open our ears
that we may hear the weeping
of the world.
Open our mouths
that we may be a voice
for the voiceless,
Open our eyes
that we may see your vision
of peace and justice.
Make us alive with the courage and faith
of your prophetic truth.
Come, Holy Spirit,
renew the whole creation.

Spirit of unity,
Reconcile your people.
Give us the wisdom
to hold to what we need
to be your church.
Give us the grace
to lay down
those things that you can do without.
Give us a vision of your breadth
and length and height
which will challenge our
smallness of heart
and bring us humbly together.
Come, Holy Spirit,
renew the whole creation.

Holy Spirit,
transform and sanctify us
as we take up this task
in your name.
Give us the gifts we need
to be your church
in spirit and in truth.
Come, Holy Spirit,
renew the whole creation.

45   O Lord Almighty,
the healer of our souls and bodies,
you put down and raise up,
you chastise and heal also;
now, in your great mercy
visit our brothers and sisters, who are sick.
Stretch forth your hand
that is full of healing and health,
and raise them up,
and cure them of their illness.

Put away from them
the spirit of disease
and of every malady, pain and fever
to which they are bound;
and if they have sins and transgressions,
grant to them remission and forgiveness, in that you love humankind;
yea, Lord my God,
pity your creation, through the compassions of your only-begotten Son,
together with your all-holy, good, and life-creating Spirit,
with whom you are blessed,
both now and ever, and to ages of ages.
Amen.

46   Remember, Lord, the city in which we dwell,
          and every city and region, and the faithful that inhabit it.

                                                                              Romania

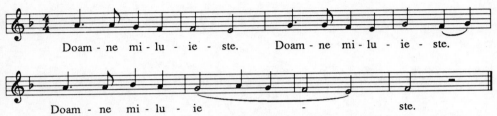

Doam - ne mi - lu - ie - ste.   Doam - ne mi - lu - ie - ste.

Doam - ne mi - lu - ie   -   ste.

Kyrie eleison. Lord have mercy. Herr, erbarme dich. Seigneur, aie pitié. Señor, ten piedad.

          Remember, Lord, them that voyage, that travel, that are sick,
          that are labouring, that are in prison, and their safety.

          Response

          Remember, Lord, them that bear fruit, and do good deeds
          in your holy churches, and that remember the poor.

          Response

          And send forth on us all the riches of your compassion,
          and grant us with one mouth and one heart to glorify and celebrate
          your glorious and majestic name, Father, Son and Holy Spirit,
          now and ever, and to ages of ages.

          Response

          And the mercies of the great God and our Saviour Jesus Christ
          shall be with us all.
          Amen.

47   Let us pray.

          Because the world is beautiful,
          and beauty is a tender thing,
          and we are stewards of creation,
          we need you, God.
          We need you, God.

          Because human knowledge seems endless,
          and we do not know what we do not know,
          we need you, God.
          We need you, God.

Because we can live without you,
and are free to go against you,
and could worship our wisdom alone,
we need you, God.
We need you, God.

Because you came among us,
and sat beside us,
and heard us speak and saw us ignore you,
and healed our pain and let us wound you,
and loved us to the end,
and triumphed over all our hatred,
we need you, God.
We need you, God.
Amen.

48   God of life, we thank you that you have set us free from the power of sin and death. You have sent us forth as signs of your kingdom into all the world. We thank you for people of grace and courage who struggle amidst the sorrows of the world to show forth your light.
Spirit of truth, set us free.

God of life, through your grace Jesus Christ has illumined our lives and all the world with his light. Enlighten our hearts that we may abound in hope. We thank you for leaders of vision and creativity who call your church to new life and hope. Inspire all people with your Spirit that they may be set free to new life and hope.
Spirit of truth, set us free.

God of life, we thank you for women and men of faith throughout history who have responded to your call to freedom and life. Open our eyes and awaken our ears to see and hear you at work in the world and in our lives. Break down the barriers that enslave and divide people and set them free to life in abundance.
Spirit of truth, set us free.

49   Spirit of peace, fill all of creation with your transforming presence. May the leaders of all countries rule with maturity and justice. May all nations have tranquility and their sons and daughters be blessed. May the people and the flocks and the herds prosper and be free from illness. May the fields bear much fruit and the land be fertile. May the face of all enemies be turned towards peace.

From "Missa da Terra Sem Males"   D. Pedro Casaldáliga, Pedro Tierra, Martin Coplas:
                                                                     Guarany, Brazil--Paraguay

Sha - lom,   sa - wi-di,   a paz.   Sha-lom,   sa - wi-di,   a paz.

Peace Friede Paix Paz

Spirit of Unity, we pray for your church. Fill it with all truth and peace.
Where it is corrupt, purify it; where it is in error, direct it; where in anything
it is amiss, reform it; where it is right, strengthen it; where it is in need,
provide for it; where it is divided, reunite it.

Response

Spirit of love, watch over those who wake or watch or weep, and give your
angels charge over those who sleep. Tend the sick, rest the weary, give
courage to women in childbirth, soothe the suffering, and bless the dying.

Response

50   In a world dominated by images of war
             set us free from the bondage of conflict.

             In a world of barriers
             set us free from the bondage of race.

             May we who once were no people
             become a living community as your people.
             Give us one heart and soul
             that we may have all things in common.

VIII. Benedictions

51   Let us pray:
             Lord Jesus Christ,
             because you broke bread with the poor,
             you were looked on with contempt.

             Because you broke bread with the sinful and outcast,
             you were looked on as ungodly.

Because you broke bread with the joyful,
you were called a winebibber and a glutton.

Because you broke bread in the upstairs room,
you sealed your acceptance of the way of the cross.

Because you broke bread on the road to Emmaus,
you made the scales fall from the disciples' eyes.
Because you broke bread and shared it,
we will do so too,
and ask your blessing.

Lord Jesus Christ,
set your blessing on the bread we break
and on the company we share.
Renew our common life,
that with each other we may share the scriptures
and feel our hearts burning within us on the road.
Amen.

52   Go with the strength you have.
Go simply
    lightly
    gently
in search of Love.
And the Spirit go with you.

53   God of power,
may the boldness of your Spirit transform us,
may the gentleness of your Spirit lead us,
may the gifts of your Spirit
equip us to serve and worship you
now and always.
Through Jesus Christ our Lord,
Amen.

54   Dear Lord, help us to persevere without stress,
to achieve without success,
to arrive without striving,
so that all that we do
brings glory to you.
Amen.

55   May God Almighty bless you,
          blessings of heaven above
          blessings of the deep lying below
          blessings of the breasts and womb
          blessings of the grain and flowers
          blessings of the eternal mountains
          bounty of the everlasting hills,
          be with you and go with you,
          in the name of the Father, Son and Holy Spirit.
          Amen.

56   Go in peace.
          And may the Holy God surprise you
          on the way,
          Christ Jesus be your company
          and the Spirit lift up your life.
          Amen.

57   May the God of Love who shared his love
                  strengthen us in our love for others.
          May the Son who shared his life
                  grant us grace that we might share our life.
          And may the Holy Spirit indwelling us
                  empower us to be
                  only and always for others.
          Amen.

58   Eternal God,
          our beginning and our end,
          be our starting point and our heaven
          and accompany us in this day's journey.
          Use our hands
          to do the work of your creation
          and use our lives
          to bring others the new life you give this world in
          Jesus Christ, Redeemer of all.
          Amen.

Ordnung für den täglichen Gottesdienst

Vorbereitung
Anrufung
Psalm oder Loblied
Sündenbekenntnis, Worte der Vergebung

Hereinbringen der Bibel
Altes Testament oder Epistellesung
Evangeliumslesung
Akklamation
Responsorien

Glaubensbekenntnisse
Fürbitten
Vaterunser

Segen

Lied

I. Anrufung

1 Gott der Gnade und der Heiligkeit,
sende uns heute deinen Heiligen Geist,
wie du ihn auch deinen Aposteln gesandt hast
am Pfingstfest,
damit unsere Gebete und unsere Taten
Zeugnis ablegen von dem einen Wunsch, der uns beseelt:
Wir möchten eins sein, o Herr,
damit die Welt glaube, dass wir dir gehören.
Erfülle uns nun mit deiner Liebe.

2 O Licht!
Göttliche und heilige Dreieinigkeit,
wir, die auf der Erde Geborenen,
preisen dich ewiglich
zusammen mit den himmlischen Heerscharen.
Lass bei Anbruch des Tages
dein klares Licht
in unsere Seelen leuchten.

3 Flamme des Heiligen Geistes,
erwärme unsere Herzen, damit wir unsere Nachbarn lieben.

Flamme des Heiligen Geistes,
erleuchte unsere Wege, damit wir in Wahrheit wandeln.

Flamme des Heiligen Geistes,
steige in uns auf, damit wir nach Freiheit verlangen.

Flamme des Heiligen Geistes,
bringe uns zusammen, damit wir deine Lebendigkeit bezeugen.

4 Himmlischer König, Tröster, du Geist der Wahrheit,
überall gegenwärtig und alles erfüllend,
Quelle alles Segens und Spender allen Lebens:
Komm und wohne in uns, reinige uns von aller Unreinheit,
und rette, du Gütiger, unsere Seelen.

3.
Pentecost / Pfingsten
Pentecôte / Pentecostés

4.
Baptism of Christ / Taufe Christi
Baptême du Christi / El Bautismo de Cristo

5   O Gott, Heiliger Geist,
komm zu uns und sei unter uns;
komm wie der Wind und mache uns rein;
komm wie das Feuer und gib uns Glut;
komm wie der Tau und erfrische uns;
überzeuge, bekehre und segne
viele Herzen und Leben
zu unserem Besten
und zu deiner Herrlichkeit.
Darum bitten wir dich um Jesu Christi willen.

6   Komm, Heiliger Geist,
entflamme unsere wartenden Herzen!

Entzünde uns mit deiner Liebe,
erneuere uns in deinem Leben.

7   Geist des Lichts: Lass deine Weisheit über uns scheinen.
Komm, Schöpfer Geist, komm in unsere Herzen, mach uns zu deiner neuen Schöpfung.

Geist des Schweigens: Lass uns Gottes Gegenwart erfahren.
(Antwort wie oben)

Geist des Mutes: Vertreibe die Furcht aus unseren Herzen.
(Antwort wie oben)

Geist des Feuers: Entflamme uns mit der Liebe Christi.
(Antwort wie oben)

Geist des Friedens: Hilf uns, zur Ruhe zu kommen und auf Gottes Wort zu hören.
(Antwort wie oben)

Geist der Freude: Begeistere uns, die gute Nachricht zu verkünden.
(Antwort wie oben)

Geist der Liebe: Hilf uns, uns den Nöten anderer zu öffnen.
(Antwort wie oben)

Geist der Stärke: Schenke uns allen deine Hilfe und Kraft.
(Antwort wie oben)

Geist der Wahrheit: Leite uns alle auf dem Weg Christi.
(Antwort wie oben)

8   Schwestern und Brüder — steht auf!
Steht auf und erhebt eure Herzen,
steht auf und erhebt eure Augen,
steht auf und erhebt eure Stimme!

Der lebendige Gott,
der lebendige, sich bewegende Geist Gottes
hat uns zusammengerufen
zum Zeugnis,
im Feiern,
zum Kampf.

Geht aufeinander zu,
denn unser Gott streckt seine Hände nach uns aus!
Lasst uns Gott anbeten!

9   Der Himmel freue sich, und die Erde sei fröhlich,
das Meer brause und was darinnen ist,
das Feld sei fröhlich und alles, was darauf ist,
es sollen jauchzen alle Bäume im Walde
vor dem Herrn, denn er kommt, zu richten das Erdreich.
Er wird den Erdkreis richten mit Gerechtigkeit
und die Völker mit seiner Wahrheit.

(Stille)

Das Werk Gottes umgibt uns.
Wir antworten mit Lobpreis.

Die Liebe Gottes ist sichtbar.
Wir antworten im Glauben.

Das Wort Gottes ruft uns.
Wir antworten in Hoffnung.

Der Wind des Geistes weht.
Wir antworten mit Freude.

10   Betet für das Ansteigen der Flüsse und Seen in diesem Jahr,
dass Christus, unser Herr,
sie segne und sie ihr Wasser über die Erde ausgiessen,
dass er dem Erdboden reichen Ertrag gewährt,
den Menschen beisteht,
das Vieh bewahrt,
und uns unsere Sünden vergibt.
Herr, erbarme dich.

Betet für die Bäume, die Pflanzenwelt
und Anpflanzungen in diesem Jahr,
dass Christus, unser Herr, sie segne,
damit sie wachsen und reichhaltig Früchte tragen,
dass er Mitleid mit seiner Schöpfung hat,
und uns unsere Sünden vergibt.
Herr, erbarme dich.

Gewähre, o Herr, der Erde Gutes,
mache sie fruchtbar
und verfüge über unser Leben, wie es dir am besten erscheint.
Kröne dieses Jahr mit deiner Güte
um der Armen deines Volkes willen.
Behüte den Fremdling, hilf den Witwen und Waisen
und stehe uns bei.
Denn unsere Augen richten sich auf dich, unsere Hoffnung,
und suchen deinen heiligen Namen.
Du sorgst für unsere Nahrung, Herr, zu gegebener Zeit.
Nimm dich unsrer an, o Herr, in deiner unendlichen Güte,
du, der du alle speist.
Erfülle unsere Herzen mit Freude und Gnade,
damit wir, da wir genug von allem haben,
in jeder guten Tat wachsen.
Amen.

II. Aufruf zum Gottesdienst

11   Die Welt gehört Gott,
die Erde und alle Völker.

Wie schön und lieblich ist es,
in Eintracht zusammenzuleben.

Liebe und Glauben begegnen sich,
Gerechtigkeit und Frieden gehen Hand in Hand.

Wenn die, die dem Herrn folgen, schweigen,
schreien diese Steine laut auf.

Herr, öffne unsere Lippen,
damit unser Mund deinen Ruhm verkünde.

12   Freut euch, ihr Völker Gottes,
feiert das Leben in euch
und Christi Gegenwart in eurer Mitte!

Unsere Augen werden aufgehen!
Die Gegenwart erhält einen neuen Sinn,
und die Zukunft wird vor Hoffnung strahlen.

Freut euch, ihr Völker Gottes,
verneigt euch vor Gott,
unserer einzigen Weisheit und Stärke.

Wir bringen uns selbst vor Gott,
damit wir, berührt von Gottes Geist,
rein werden.

13   Im Geheimen und in der Grösse
erscheint uns das Angesicht Gottes,
im Irdischen und dem Unscheinbaren
erfahren wir die Liebe Christi.

Überall, auf den Höhen und in den Tiefen,
im Leben und auch im Tod
ist es der Geist Gottes,
der uns begegnet.

Lasst uns Gott loben.

14   Ich will ein Licht anzünden,
im Namen Gottes,
der die Welt erleuchtet
und mir den Odem des Lebens eingehaucht hat.

Ich will ein Licht anzünden
im Namen des Sohnes,
der die Welt errettet
und mir seine Hand gereicht hat.

Ich will ein Licht anzünden
im Namen des Heiligen Geistes,
der die Welt umfasst
und meine Seele mit Verlangen erfüllt.

*Wir werden drei Lichter anzünden
für den dreieinigen Gott der Liebe:*

*Gott über uns,
Gott neben uns
Gott unter uns,
von Anfang
bis ans Ende,
bis in die Ewigkeit.*

15   Schwestern und Brüder,
wir sind hier zusammengekommen,
um Gott, der uns Freiheit schenkt, zu preisen
durch Jesus Christus, unseren Herrn.
Denn der lebenspendende Geist in Jesus Christus
hat uns befreit von dem Gesetz der Sünde und des Todes.
*Denn wir haben nicht einen knechtischen Geist empfangen,
dass wir uns abermals fürchten müssen,
sondern wir haben den Geist
der Kinder Gottes empfangen.*

16   Wir preisen voller Ehrfurcht
das Geheimnis, Gott den Vater,
die Antwort, Gott den Sohn,
das Zeugnis, Gott den Heiligen Geist.
Wir beten an die Heilige Dreieinigkeit
drei Gestalten in einer.

III. Lobpreis und Anbetung

17   Herr Jesus, wie eine Mutter sammelst du dein Volk um dich:
du meinst es gut mit uns wie eine Mutter mit ihren Kindern.

Oft weinst du um unsere Sünden und unseren Stolz:
sanft entziehst du uns dem Hass und der Strafe.

Du tröstest uns im Kummer und verbindest unsere Wunden:
in Krankheit pflegst du uns, mit reiner Milch ernährst du uns.

Herr Jesus, durch deinen Tod werden wir zu neuem Leben geboren:
durch dein Leiden und deine Wehen kommen wir in Freude hervor.

Durch deine grosse Güte wandelt sich Verzweiflung in Hoffnung:
durch deine Sanftmut finden wir Trost in der Furcht.

Deine Wärme bringt den Toten Leben:
deine Berührung bringt den Sündern Gerechtigkeit.

Herr Jesus, heile uns in deiner Barmherzigkeit:
deine Liebe und deine Güte erneuern uns.

In deinem Mitleiden bring uns Gnade und Vergebung:
möge deine Liebe uns auf die Herrlichkeit des Himmels vorbereiten.

Ein Lied des Heiligen Anselm

18   Bevor die Welt geschaffen wurde
und nachdem die Ewigkeit vergangen sein wird,
bist du Gott.

Vom Meer, das über seine Ufer tritt,
bis zum Wind, der aufhört zu wehen,
bist du Gott.

In der Beständigkeit alles Geschaffenen
und in seiner Unbeständigkeit,
bist du Gott.

In der Weite des Universums
und in den vergessenen Winkeln unserer Herzen,
bist du Gott,
Du bist unser Gott,
und wir preisen dich.

19   Lobpreis sei dir, allmächtiger Gott!
Du sprachst, und Licht kam aus der Finsternis,
Ordnung kam aus dem Chaos.

(Frauen):
Du hast Odem in den Staub der Erde gehaucht,
und wir wurden nach deinem Bild geformt.

(Männer):
Du hast das Werk deiner Hände betrachtet,
und erklärtest es für gut.

Und noch sprichst, atmest und schaust du nach uns.
Wir preisen dich!

Lobpreis sei dir, Herr Jesus Christ!
Du trafst uns als Flüchtling, als bedrohtes Kind,
das Wort wurde zu Mensch, an einem verborgenen Ort geboren.

(Frauen:)
Du riefst uns mit Namen, das zu verlassen, was behaglich war,
um dir Jüngerinnen, Gefährtinnen und Freundinnen zu sein.

(Männer:)
Du hast uns gerettet, indem du zu unseren Füssen knietest,
indem du deine Arme weit ausgebreitet hast,
um unsere Sünden auf dich zu nehmen,
indem du durch den Tod wieder zum Leben kamst.

Und noch triffst, rufst und rettest du uns.
Wir preisen dich!

Lobpreis sei dir, Heiliger Geist!
Du hast über das Chaos nachgedacht,
Gottes neue Schöpfung geformt und bemuttert.

(Frauen:)
Du hast Prophetinnen und Glaubensboten inspiriert,
um für jede Situation das rechte Wort zu finden.

(Männer:)
Du hast die Urkirche zur Mission befreit,
indem du alles Leben für den Herrn des Universums beansprucht hast.

Und noch denkst du nach über uns, erleuchtest und befreist uns.
Wir preisen dich!

Ehre sei dir, Dreieiniger Gott!
Du bist vom Gesang der Heiligen im Himmel umgeben,
und doch bist du unter uns.
Wir beten dich an!

20

Ich sah das Wasser über die Schwelle des Tempels fliessen:
wo der Fluss überfliesst, entspringt überall Leben.

An den Ufern des Flusses wachsen Bäume,
die alle möglichen Früchte tragen:
weder werden ihre Blätter welken noch ihre Früchte ausbleiben.

Ihre Früchte werden als Nahrung dienen,
ihre Blätter werden die Völker heilen:
denn der Fluss des Lebenswassers fliesst
aus dem Throne Gottes und des Lammes.

IV. Bekenntnis

21

Herr, deine Wege sind nicht unsere Wege;
deine Gedanken sind nicht unsere Gedanken;
was uns eine Ewigkeit erscheint,
ist nur ein Augenblick für dich.

Hilf uns, angesichts der Ewigkeit
demütig zu sein.

Traditional Urdu   R.F. Liberius: Pakistan

1. Khu- da- ya, ra- hem kar. Khu- da- ya, ra- hem,
Have mer - cy on us, Lord, have mer - cy on us.

Khu- da- ya, ra- hem kar. Khu- da- ya, ra- hem.
Have mer - cy on us, Lord, have mer - cy on us.

Khu — da - ya, ra - hem kar, khu - da - ya, ra - hem.
Have mer - cy on us, Lord, have mer - cy on us.

Kyrie eleison. Herr, erbarme dich. Seigneur, aie pitié de nous. Señor, ten piedad de nosotros.
Christe eleison. Christe, erbarme dich. O Christ, aie pitié de nous. Christo, ten piedad de nosotros.

Wenn wir Lobpreis mit unseren Stimmen gesungen
aber die Freude aus unseren Herzen verbannt haben;

wenn wir nur um das Mögliche gebetet
und nur auf das Sichtbare gehofft haben;

wenn wir deine Gnade für selbstverständlich gehalten
und umgehende Antworten auf eben gestellte Fragen erwartet haben;

wenn wir es zugelassen haben,
dass unser Warten auf deinen Geist erlahmte
und Beten ein Ersatz für Handeln wurde;

wenn wir unsere Gedanken nur darauf ausgerichtet haben,
wie wir auf dich harren, und nie darauf, wie du auf uns wartest:

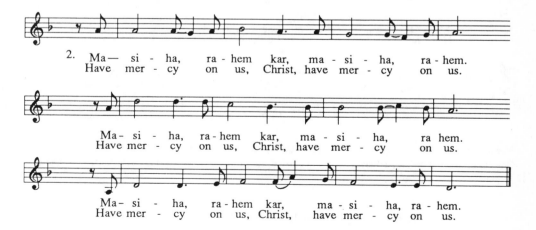

2. Ma — si - ha, ra - hem kar, ma - si - ha, ra - hem.
Have mer - cy on us, Christ, have mer - cy on us.

Ma - si - ha, ra - hem kar, ma - si - ha, ra hem.
Have mer - cy on us, Christ, have mer - cy on us.

Ma - si - ha, ra - hem kar, ma - si - ha, ra - hem.
Have mer - cy on us, Christ, have mer - cy on us.

Kyrie eleison. Herr, erbarme dich. Seigneur, aie pitié de nous. Señor, ten piedad de nosotros.
Christe eleison. Christe, erbarme dich. O Christ, aie pitié de nous. Christo, ten piedad de nosotros.

Wenn wir gebetet haben, "Spender des Lebens, erhalte deine Schöpfung"
und dem Konsum erlegen sind.

Wenn wir gebetet haben, "Geist der Wahrheit — mache uns frei"
und stattdessen die Sklaverei des Schweigens gewählt haben.

Wenn wir gebetet haben, "Geist der Einheit — versöhne dein Volk"
und nicht mit Menschen anderen Glaubens oder anderer Traditionen in
unserer Nachbarschaft zusammengekommen sind.

Wenn wir gebetet haben, "Heiliger Geist - wandle und heilige uns"
und nicht selber erwartet haben, dass der Geist unser Leben ändert.

Traditional Urdu   R.F. Liberius: Pakistan

3. Khu-da-ya, ra-hem kar. Khu-da-ya, ra-hem,
Have mer-cy on us, Lord, have mer-cy on us.

Khu-da-ya, ra-hem kar. Khu-da-ya, ra-hem.
Have mer-cy on us, Lord, have mer-cy on us.

Khu—da-ya, ra-hem kar, khu-da-ya, ra-hem.
Have mer-cy on us, Lord, have mer-cy on us.

Kyrie eleison. Herr, erbarme dich. Seigneur, aie pitié de nous. Señor, ten piedad de nosotros.
Christe eleison. Christe, erbarme dich. O Christ, aie pitié de nous. Christo, ten piedad de nosotros.

Hört, denn dies ist wahrhaftig Gottes Wort:
Gesegnet sind alle, die des Herrn harren.
Gott ist barmherzig, und Gottes Liebe ist stark und mächtig.
Amen.

22 Geist der Freude,
durch deine Gegenwart lebt Christus in uns
und wir in ihm:
Vergib uns, wenn wir dich vergessen
und wenn es uns nicht gelingt,
aus deiner Freude heraus unser Leben zu gestalten.
Geist Gottes, vergib uns
und führe uns zum Leben in dir.

Geist der Liebe,
du verbindest uns in Liebe mit dir
und mit den Menschen um uns herum,
in Partnerschaft, in Familie, in Freundschaft.
Vergib uns, wenn wir diejenigen verletzen, die wir lieben,
und wenn wir uns von ihrer Liebe abwenden.
Geist Gottes, vergib uns
und führe uns zum Leben in dir.

Geist des Leibes Christi,
verbinde uns in einer Kirche
durch deine lebenspendende Gnade und Hoffnung.
Vergib uns unser Stückwerk beim Aufbau deiner Kirche
und unser Versagen, deine Liebe in die Welt hineinzutragen.
Geist Gottes, vergib uns
und führe uns zum Leben in dir.

Geist in der Welt,
du tröstest uns
und bringst uns einander näher.
Vergib uns unsere Kriege und unseren Hass,
vergib uns unser Versagen, dich zu erkennen in allen Menschen.
Geist Gottes, vergib uns
und führe uns zum Leben in dir.

Nehmt an das Geschenk des Friedens
wie die Taube, die sich sanft auf dem Baum niederlässt.
Nehmt an das Geschenk des Lebens
wie die Flamme, die frei aufsteigt, hell und warm.
Nehmt an das Geschenk des Heiligen Geistes
wie der Wind, der tanzend über den ganzen Erdkreis weht.
Amen.

23 Herr Jesus Christus,
Sohn des lebendigen Gottes,
Sei mir Sünder
gnädig.

24   Du hast uns vom Tod befreit,
             wir preisen dich!
             Entsende uns mit dem Brot des Lebens,
             wir bitten dich!

             Du hast uns zur Umkehr gebracht,
             wir preisen dich!
             Erhalte uns im rechten Glauben,
             wir bitten dich!

             Du hast mit dem Wirken deiner Gnade begonnen,
             wir preisen dich!
             Vollende dein Heil in uns,
             wir bitten dich!

             Du hast uns zu deinem Volk gemacht,
             wir preisen dich!
             Mach uns eins mit allen Menschen,
             wir bitten dich!

25   Im Glauben
             lasst uns vor Gott treten
             und erkennen, wer wir sind:
             (stilles Gebet)

             Wir sind die Menschen, denen ein neuer Himmel
             und eine neue Erde verheissen sind,
             aber in unserem Leben erfüllen wir diese Verheissung bei weitem nicht.

             Wir sind die Menschen,
             die die Barmherzigkeit Gottes erfahren,
             aber wir versagen, wenn wir sie anderen gewähren sollen.

             Bitte und du wirst empfangen,
             suche und du wirst finden,
             klopfe an und das Leben wird sich dir eröffnen.
             Stehe auf und lebe in Freiheit und im Glauben.
             Amen.

26

Heiliger Geist, Du Fürsprecher und Trösterin,
in Dir feiern wir die befreiende Gegenwart des lebendigen Christus.
Du wehst, wo Du es willst, erfrischend, erneuernd und belebend.
Wie Feuer reinigst Du.

Heiliger Geist, Du Fürsprecher und Trösterin,
Du stellst bloss was in der Welt böse ist,
Du überführst die sündige Welt,
Wie Feuer reinigst Du.

Reinige uns, hilf uns über unsere eigenen engstirnigen Sorgen
hinauszublicken.
Erhalte, bewahre und beschütze Deine Schöpfung.
Ernähre, stütze und lenke Deine Geschöpfe.
Heiliger Geist, Du Fürsprecher und Trösterin
Wie Feuer reinigst Du uns.
Wir bitten Dich, reinige uns.

27

Lasst uns bekennen
die heimlichen Sünden, die wir ängstlich
verbergen in unserem Leben,
die uns gefangenhalten in Furcht und Schmerz,
die uns von Gott und von unseren Mitmenschen trennen.

(Stille)

Korean   Jacques Berthier: Taizé France

Chu-yo chu-yo tu-ro chu-so-so. Chu-yo chu—yo tu-ro chu-so-so.

Lord hear us. Höre uns, Gott. Ecoute nous, Dieu. Seigneur, aie pitié. Señor, escúchanos.

Lasst uns bekennen
das Stummsein, wenn es darum geht, Ungerechtigkeiten anzuklagen,
die Kompromisse, die wir eingegangen sind, die das Böse vermehren,
deren Ertrag Tod und Zerstörung sind.

(Stille)

Korean   Jacques Berthier: Taizé France

Chu-yo   chu - yo   tu-ro   chu-so-so.   Chu-yo   chu— yo   tu-ro   chu-so-so.

Lord hear us. Höre uns, Gott. Ecoute nous, Dieu. Seigneur, aie pitié. Señor, escúchanos.

Lasst uns bekennen
die Selbstzufriedenheit, mit der wir unser Leben in Uneinigkeit führen,
die Arglosigkeit, mit der wir unsere Vorurteile erhalten
und mit denen wir es ablehnen, die Menschen zu werden, für die Jesus
gebetet hat.

(Stille)

Responsorium

Gott, dem nichts verborgen bleibt
und der unsere Herzen kennt,
vergibt uns unsere Sünden
und verkündet uns die freudige Wahrheit,
dass wir befreit sind.

V. Kollektengebete

28   Geist der Wahrheit und des Urteils,
          du allein kannst die Mächte austreiben,
          die die Herrschaft der Welt an sich gerissen haben.
          Im Moment der Krise
          gib uns deine Unterscheidungskraft,
          damit wir das, was böse ist, genau benennen können
          und den Weg erkennen, der zum Frieden führt,
          durch Jesus Christus.
          Amen.

29   O Gott, unsere Unruhe,
          deine Rede ist machtvoll,
          und dein Wort wird erfüllt werden;
          lass uns erkennen, dass uns all das unbefriedigt lässt,
          was deine Wahrheit verzerrt,

und mache unsere Herzen wach,
für deine befreiende Stimme,
in Jesus Christus,
Amen.

30

Allmächtiger Gott, dein Schöpfungswort
füllte das Wasser
mit vielerlei Lebewesen
und die Luft mit Vögeln.
Wir freuen uns an dem Reichtum deiner Schöpfung
und bitten um deine Weisheit für alle,
die auf dieser Erde leben,
dass wir klug umgehen mit dem, was du für uns und für unsere Nachkommen
geschaffen hast,
und es nicht zerstören.
In Jesu Namen bitten wir dich.
Amen.

31

Gott, unser Schöpfer,
du hast uns alles geschenkt,
was wir sind und haben:
Befreie uns von Eigensucht
und befähige uns zu teilen,
was wir sind,
was wir wissen,
was wir haben,
untereinander
[in dieser Vollversammlung] und mit der von dir geliebten Welt
in Christi Namen,
der dies Teilen möglich macht.
Amen.

32

Geist der Stärke und der Veränderung,
in deiner Kraft Jesus einst kam,
damit die Völker eine Hoffnung hatten,
lass dich auch herab auf uns
frei und ausnahmslos,
damit wir Kraft und Zuversicht gewinnen,
im Geiste Jesu Christi
deine Gerechtigkeit auf Erden zu säen.
Amen.

VI. Glaubensbekenntnisse

33   Wir glauben an den einen Gott,
den Vater, den Allmächtigen,
der alles geschaffen hat, Himmel und Erde,
die sichtbare und die unsichtbare Welt.

Wir glauben an den einen Herrn Jesus Christus,
Gottes eingeborenen Sohn,
aus dem Vater geboren vor aller Zeit,
Licht vom Licht,
wahrer Gott vom wahren Gott,
gezeugt, nicht geschaffen,
eines Wesens mit dem Vater;
durch ihn ist alles geschaffen.
Für uns Menschen und zu unserem Heil ist er vom Himmel gekommen,
hat Fleisch angenommen durch den Heiligen Geist
von der Jungfrau Maria
und ist Mensch geworden.
Er wurde für uns gekreuzigt unter Pontius Pilatus,
hat gelitten und ist begraben worden,
ist am dritten Tage auferstanden nach der Schrift
und aufgefahren in den Himmel.

Er sitzt zur Rechten des Vaters
und wird wiederkommen in Herrlichkeit,
zu richten die Lebenden und die Toten;
seiner Herrschaft wird kein Ende sein.

Wir glauben an den Heiligen Geist,
der Herr ist und lebendig macht,
der aus dem Vater hervorgeht;
der mit dem Vater und dem Sohn
angebetet und verherrlicht wird,
der gesprochen hat durch die Propheten;
und die eine, heilige, katholische und apostolische Kirche.
Wir bekennen die eine Taufe zur Vergebung der Sünden.
Wir erwarten die Auferstehung der Toten
und das Leben der kommenden Welt.
Amen.

Glaubensbekenntnis von Nizäa — Konstantinopel

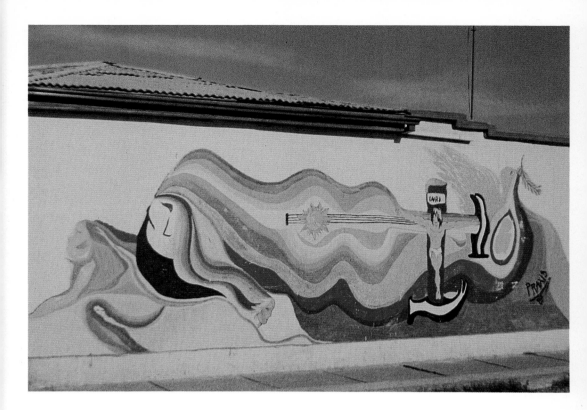

Spirit in action / Das Wirken des Geistes
L'Esprit à l'oeuvre / El Espíritu en acción

6.
Pentecost / Pfingsten
Pentecôte / Pentecostés

34   Ich glaube an Gott,
den Vater, den Allmächtigen,
den Schöpfer des Himmels und der Erde.

Ich glaube an Jesus Christus,
seinen eingeborenen Sohn,
unseren Herrn,
empfangen durch den Heiligen Geist,
geboren von der Jungfrau Maria,
gelitten unter Pontius Pilatus,
gekreuzigt, gestorben
und begraben,
hinabgestiegen in das Reich des Todes,
am dritten Tage
auferstanden von den Toten,
aufgefahren in den Himmel;
er sitzt zur Rechten Gottes,
des allmächtigen Vaters;
von dort wird er kommen,
zu richten die Lebenden und die Toten.

Ich glaube an den Heiligen Geist,
die heilige christliche Kirche,
Gemeinschaft der Heiligen,
Vergebung der Sünden,
Auferstehung der Toten
und das ewige Leben.
Amen.

Das Apostolische Glaubensbekenntnis

VII. Fürbittgebete

35   Gott, unser Vater,
bewahre unsere Küsten vor den Waffen des Todes,
und unser Land vor allem, was den jungen Menschen Liebe und Freiheit
verwehrt.
Lass die Meere [des Pazifischen Ozeans]
Botschaften des Friedens und Wohlwollens weitertragen.
Vertreibe aus unserer Mitte Unfreundlichkeit und Gewalt.
Lass unsere Kinder schwimmen und frische Luft atmen,
die erfüllt ist vom Heiligen Geist.

Herr Jesus,
segne alle, die den inneren Frieden schaffen,
der die Schranken des Hasses durchbricht,
und vereinige uns mit den offenen Armen deines Kreuzes,
damit die Völker der Welt glücklich zusammenleben.
Amen.

36   O Gott,
du spendest Leben,
wir bitten dich für die Kirche in der ganzen Welt:
Heilige ihr Leben, erneuere ihren Gottesdienst;
gib ihrem Zeugnis Kraft;
richte ihre Einheit wieder auf,
stärke diejenigen, die zusammen den Gehorsam im Glauben suchen,
der uns verbindet.
Heile die Spaltungen, durch die deine Kinder voneinander getrennt sind,
damit sie die Einheit des Geistes
durch das Band des Friedens bewahren.
Amen.

37   O Gott,
du liebst die Gerechtigkeit und richtest in der Welt den Frieden auf,
wir bringen die Zwietracht unserer heutigen Welt vor dich:
sinnlose Gewalt und Kriege, die die Zuversicht der Menschen zerstören;
Militarismus und Wettrüsten, die das Leben der Welt bedrohen;
menschliche Begierde und Ungerechtigkeit, die Hass und Konflikte
mit sich bringen.
Sende deinen Geist und erneuere das Gesicht der Erde:
Lehre uns, Mitleid mit der menschlichen Familie zu haben;
stärke den Willen all derer, die sich für Frieden und Gerechtigkeit einsetzen;
führe die Völker auf den Pfad des Friedens
und gib du uns den Frieden, den die Welt nicht geben kann.
Amen.

38   Herr, durch das vergossene Blut deiner Heiligen
führe die zerstreuten Kinder deiner Kirche und alle in Freude zusammen,
die bitterlich über die Traurigkeit der Entzweiung weinen.
Du schenkst uns die Gnade der Erlösung.

39   Lasst uns Gott anrufen um das Kommen des Gottesreiches.

O Gott, lindere den Schmerz der Gefolterten
mit deinem Frieden.

Stille den Hunger der Allerärmsten
mit deiner Fülle.

Verbinde die Wunden unseres Planeten
mit deinem Heilsein.

Was Tod ist,
erwecke mit deinem Lebensatem.

Denen, die sich nach dir sehnen,
gewähre dich selbst.

Dein Reich komme,
dein Wille geschehe,
*Dein ist das Reich, die Kraft und die Herrlichkeit
in Ewigkeit.*

Unser Gott ist bei uns.

Wir feiern das Wunder des Lebens und Seins!
Wir feiern das Wunder der Schöpfung!
Unser Gott hat uns lieb.
Gottes Segen liegt auf unserem Leben,
lasst uns mit Freuden Gott danken.
Amen.

40   Da wir heute an dem Leben deiner Kirche Anteil haben,
beten wir darum, dass unser Zeugnis in der Wahrheit Christi stehe.
Gib uns eine Stimme für die, die keine Stimme haben.
Und stille Gemeinschaft,
wenn nur Schweigen dem Schmerz angemessen ist.

Gib uns Tränen angesichts des Kummers.
Und Lachen, wenn wir die Freuden deiner Schöpfung erfahren.

Gib uns einen scharfen Sinn, um Ungerechtigkeiten aufzudecken.
Und beständige Nachsicht mit denen,
die uns als Verzweifelte begegnen.

Gib uns Ehrlichkeit, damit wir unsere Ratlosigkeit eingestehen können.
Und Treue im Zusammenleben mit unseren Mitmenschen,
denn du berufst uns dazu, mit dir im Vertrauen zu wirken. Darum
vertrauen wir darauf, dass in unseren Gebeten unsere Liebe mit
deiner Liebe für die Welt zusammenfliesst.

In der Gnade Gottes liegen unendliche Möglichkeiten der Hoffnung.
Amen.

41   Gedenke, Herr, des herabfallenden Regens, der Gewässer und Flüsse und
segne sie.

Gedenke, Herr, der Pflanzen, der Saat und der Früchte des Feldes, segne sie
und lass sie unter deinem Segen reichlich gedeihen.

Gedenke, Herr, der Sicherheit deiner eigenen heiligen Kirche und aller
Städte und Länder.

Gedenke, Herr, der Sicherheit der Menschen und Tiere und der sündhaften
Menschen, die dir dienen.

Gedenke, Herr, unserer Väter und Mütter, unserer Schwestern und Brüder, die
entschlafen sind und im rechten Glauben zu ihrer lezten Ruhe gegangen sind.

Gedenke, Herr, der Gefangenen deines Volkes und bringe sie in Frieden
heim.

Gedenke, Herr, der Notleidenden und Betrübten.

Gedenke, Herr, derer, die dir dienen; der Armen, die Unterdrückung leiden,
erbarme dich ihrer und erhalte sie im rechten Glauben; und lass den Heiligen
Geist in ihnen wohnen, durch unsere geistliche Freude und die Liebe der
Menschheit.
Amen.

42   O Gott, sei gegenwärtig unter uns, unter uns Menschen auf der Erde.
Öffne unsere Augen für das Heil, das in dir ist,
offenbare dich der verblendeten Menschheit.

Lasse dein Angesicht leuchten über denen, die durch Krankheit nieder-
geworfen sind. Gib ihnen deine Zuversicht und deinen Frieden.

Verleih den Armen und Schwachen und allen,
auf denen das Elend schwer lastet,
deine Zuversicht und deinen Frieden. Gib ihnen deine Erkenntnis und sei ihr
Halt, damit sie von dir erfüllt werden.

Gewähre den Mächtigen und Reichen die Macht, die sie nicht haben.
Gib ihnen die Weisheit zu unterscheiden, damit sie frei sind durch deine
Freiheit, frei zu lieben.

Gib uns allen deinen Frieden und deine Lebenskraft.
Amen.

43 Wo Unwissenheit, Selbstliebe und Unverständnis das Leben
in der Gemeinschaft zerbrochen haben,
schenk dein Licht, Gott der Liebe.

Wo Ungerechtigkeit und Unterdrückung den Lebenswillen
der Völker gebrochen haben,
schenk dein Licht, Gott der Befreiung.

Wo Hunger und Armut, Krankheit und Tod das Leben
zu einer unerträglichen Last gemacht haben,
schenk dein Licht, Gott der Gnade.

Wo Misstrauen und Hass, Streit und Krieg
deine Güte zunichte gemacht haben,
schenk dein Licht, Gott des Friedens.

Ewiger Gott,
nimm die Blindheit von den Nationen und Völkern,
auf dass sie im Licht der Liebe wandeln mögen;
nimm die Unwissenheit und Verstocktheit von den Nationen und Völkern,
damit sie von der Quelle deiner Güte trinken mögen.
Amen.

44 Komm, Heiliger Geist, erneuere die ganze Schöpfung,
sende den Wind und die Flamme deines Lebens, das verwandelt,
um die Kirche heute aufzurichten.
Gewähre uns Weisheit und Glauben,
damit wir um die grosse Hoffnung wissen,
zu der wir berufen sind.
Komm, Heiliger Geist,
erneuere die ganze Schöpfung.

Spender des Lebens, erhalte deine Schöpfung.
Konfrontiere uns mit
unserer zerstörerischen Gier nach deinen Gaben.
Stehe vor uns,
wenn wir plündern und zerstören.
Rufe uns auf
zu neuer Harmonie aus Verantwortung
für alles, was lebt und atmet
und besteht.
Komm, Heiliger Geist,
erneuere die ganze Schöpfung.

Geist der Wahrheit,
mache uns frei,
um Kinder Gottes zu werden.
Öffne unsere Ohren,
damit wir das Weinen und Wehklagen
der Welt hören.
Öffne unsere Lippen,
damit wir eine Stimme sein mögen für die,
die keine Stimme haben.
Öffne unsere Augen,
damit wir deine Vision
des Friedens und der Gerechtigkeit sehen.
Erfülle uns mit Mut und Glauben,
die deiner prophetischen Wahrheit entspringen.
Komm, Heiliger Geist,
erneuere die ganze Schöpfung.

Geist der Einheit,
versöhne dein Volk.
Gib uns Weisheit,
das zu bewahren, was wir brauchen,
um deine Kirche zu sein.

Gib uns Gnade,
um Dinge aufzugeben,
ohne die du auskommen kannst.
Schenke uns eine Offenbarung deiner Grösse
und deiner Herrlichkeit,
die unser kleinliches Herz herausfordert
und uns in Demut zusammenbringt.
Komm, Heiliger Geist,
erneuere die ganze Schöpfung.

Heiliger Geist,
wandle und heilige uns,
wenn wir in deinem Namen
auf diese Aufgaben zugehen.
Gib uns die Gaben, die wir brauchen,
um deine Kirche
im Geist und in der Wahrheit zu sein.
Komm, Heiliger Geist,
erneuere die ganze Schöpfung.

45   Allmächtiger Gott,
Heiler unserer Seelen und unseres Leibes,
du züchtigst und tötest nicht,
mögest du in deiner grossen Barmherzigkeit
unsere Schwestern und Brüder besuchen,
die krank daniederliegen.
Reiche uns deine Hand,
voll von Gesundheit und Heilung,
lass die Kranken aufstehen
und wende alle Krankheit von ihnen ab.

Wehre dem Geist der Krankheit,
lindere den Schmerz, lösche das Fieber,
vertreibe alle verborgene Schwachheit,
und wenn sie gesündigt und sich vergangen haben,
gewähre ihnen Erlass der Sünden und Vergebung,
weil du die Menschheit liebst:
O Herr, mein Gott,
erbarme dich deiner Schöpfung
durch das Leiden deines eingeborenen Sohns,
gemeinsam mit dem allheiligen, guten und lebendigmachenden Geist,
jetzt und immerdar,
und von Ewigkeit zu Ewigkeit.
Amen.

46   Gedenke, Herr, der Stadt, in der wir wohnen,
jeder Stadt und jedes Landes, und der Gläubigen, die darin wohnen.

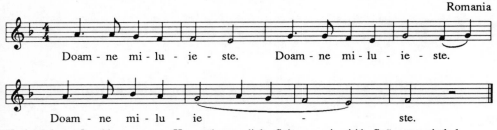

Doam - ne mi - lu - ie - ste.   Doam - ne mi - lu - ie - ste.

Doam - ne mi - lu - ie   ste.

Kyrie eleison. Lord have mercy. Herr, erbarme dich. Seigneur, aie pitié. Señor, ten piedad.

Gedenke, Herr, der Reisenden, der Kranken, der Leidenden, Gefangenen
und beschütze sie.

Responsorium

Gedenke, Herr, derer, die Gaben und Wohltaten hervorbringen in deinen
heiligen Kirchen und die der Armen nicht vergessen.

Responsorium

Lass über uns kommen den Reichtum deiner Barmherzigkeit
und lass uns mit einem Mund und einem Herzen deinen herrlichen und hohen
Namen preisen und feiern, Vater, Sohn und Heiliger Geist,
jetzt und immerdar und von Ewigkeit zu Ewigkeit.

Responsorium

Und die Gnade des grossen Gottes und Heilands
Jesus Christus sei mit uns allen.
Amen.

47   Lass uns beten:

Weil die Welt schön ist,
und Schönheit etwas Zerbrechliches ist,
und wir die Haushalter deiner Schöpfung sind,
brauchen wir dich, o Gott.
Wir brauchen dich, o Gott.

Weil menschliches Wissen grenzenlos scheint,
und wir nicht wissen, was wir nicht wissen,
brauchen wir dich, o Gott.
Wir brauchen dich, o Gott.

Weil wir ohne dich leben können
und frei sind, uns gegen dich zu stellen,
und nur unserer Weisheit dienen könnten,
brauchen wir dich, o Gott.
Wir brauchen dich, o Gott.

Weil du zu uns gekommen bist,
und neben uns sassest,
und uns sprechen hörtest und sahst, dass wir dich nicht erkannt haben,
und unsere Schmerzen geheilt hast und dich von uns verwunden liessest,
und uns bis ans Ende liebtest,
und über unseren Hass den Sieg davon getragen hast,
brauchen wir dich, o Gott.
Wir brauchen dich, o Gott.
Amen.

48 Gott des Lebens, wir danken dir, dass du uns befreit hast von der Macht der Sünde und des Todes. Als Zeichen deines Reiches hast du uns in die Welt gesandt. Wir danken dir für Menschen voller Leidenschaft und Stärke, die inmitten der leidenden Welt darum kämpfen, dein Licht weiterzutragen.
Geist der Wahrheit, mach uns frei.

Gott des Lebens, durch dein Erbarmen hat Jesus Christus unser Leben und das der Welt mit seinem Licht erhellt. Erleuchte unsere Herzen, damit sie überfliessen von Hoffnung. Wir danken dir für Menschen, die mit Weitblick und Tatkraft deine Kirche zu neuem Leben und neuer Hoffnung rufen. Erfülle alle Menschen mit deinem Geist, damit sie befreit werden zu neuem Leben und neuer Hoffnung.
Geist der Wahrheit, mach uns frei.

Gott des Lebens, wir danken dir für Frauen und Männer, die mit ihrem Glauben auf deinen Ruf zur Freiheit und zum Leben geantwortet haben. Öffne unsere Augen und Ohren, damit wir dein Wirken in der Welt und in unsrem Leben sehen und hören. Reiss die Mauern nieder, die Menschen zu Sklaven werden lassen und sie voneinander trennen. Ermögliche ihnen ein Leben in Fülle.
Geist der Wahrheit, mach uns frei.

49 Geist des Friedens, erfülle die ganze Schöpfung mit deiner verändernden Gegenwart. Lass die Regierungen in allen Ländern ihre Entscheidungen mit Reife und Gerechtigkeit treffen. Lass alle Nationen in Ruhe leben und segne ihre Töchter und Söhne. Lass die Menschen und Tiere zahlreich und frei von Krankheit sein. Lass die Felder viele Früchte tragen und lass die Erde fruchtbar sein. Lass alle Feindschaft sich verwandeln in Frieden.

From "Missa da Terra Sem Males"   D. Pedro Casaldáliga, Pedro Tierra, Martin Coplas:
                                                    Guarany, Brazil--Paraguay

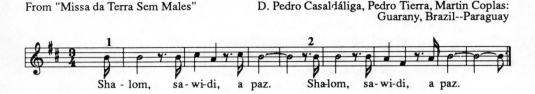

Sha - lom,   sa - wi-di,   a paz.   Sha-lom,   sa - wi-di,   a paz.

Peace Friede Paix Paz

Geist der Einheit, wir beten für deine Kirche. Erfülle sie mit Wahrheit und
Frieden. Wo sie korrupt und verdorben ist, reinige sie. Wo sie in die Irre
geht, lenke sie auf den richtigen Weg. Wo sie verkehrt handelt, verbessere
sie; wo sie das Richtige tut, stärke sie; wo sie in der Not ist, sorge für sie; wo
sie getrennt ist, bringe sie wieder zusammen.

Responsorium

Geist der Liebe, behüte die Menschen, die schlaflos sind, auf etwas warten
oder weinen, und wache über die, die schlafen. Kümmere dich um die
Kranken, den Erschöpften gib neue Kraft. Ermutige die Frauen, die Kinder
gebären, beruhige die Leidenden und segne die Sterbenden.

Responsorium

50   In einer Welt, die von Bildern des Krieges beherrscht wird,
        mach uns frei von der Knechtschaft des Konfliktes.

        In einer Welt von Barrieren,
        mach uns frei von der Knechtschaft des Rassismus.

        Lass uns, die wir einst kein Volk waren,
        zu einer lebendigen Gemeinschaft als dein Volk werden.
        Gewähre uns ein Herz und eine Seele,
        damit wir Gemeinsamkeit haben.

VIII. Segen

51   Lasst uns beten:
        Herr Jesus Christus,
        weil du das Brot mit den Armen gebrochen hast,
        wurdest du verachtet.

        Weil du das Brot mit den Sündern und Ausgestossenen gebrochen hast,
        nannte man dich gottlos.

Weil du das Brot mit fröhlichen Menschen gebrochen hast,
nannte man dich einen Weinsäufer und Fresser.

Weil du das Brot im Obergemach gebrochen hast,
nahmst du den Kreuzesweg endgültig auf dich.

Weil du das Brot auf dem Weg nach Emmaus gebrochen hast,
liessest du die Schuppen von den Augen der Jünger fallen.
Weil du das Brot gebrochen und geteilt hast,
tun auch wir es
und erbitten deinen Segen.

Herr Jesus Christus,
segne das Brot, das wir brechen,
und die Gemeinschaft, die wir miteinander teilen.
Erneuere unser gemeinsames Leben,
auf dass wir die Heilige Schrift miteinander teilen und fühlen,
wie unsere Herzen auf dem Weg miteinander brennen.
Amen.

52
Geht in der Kraft, die euch gegeben ist,
geht einfach,
    geht leichtfüssig,
    geht zart,
und haltet Ausschau nach der Liebe,
und Gottes Geist geleite euch!

53
Gott der Stärke,
möge die Kühnheit deines Geistes uns verwandeln,
möge die Güte deines Geistes uns führen,
mögen die Gaben deines Geistes
uns befähigen, dir zu dienen und dich anzubeten
jetzt und immerdar.
Durch Jesus Christus, unseren Herrn.
Amen.

54
O Herr, erhalte uns auf unserem Wege ohne Druck und Hetze,
dass wir uns einsetzen, ohne unter Erfolgszwang zu stehen,
dass wir das Ende erreichen, ohne getrieben zu sein,
dass all unser Tun
deine Ehre vermehre.
Amen.

55   Der allmächtige Gott segne euch,
mit Segen oben vom Himmel herab,
mit Segen von der Flut, die drunten liegt,
mit Segen der Brüste und des Mutterleibes,
mit Segen von dem Samenkorn und den Blumen.
Mögen die Segnungen der ewigen Berge
und die köstlichen Güter der ewigen Hügel
mit euch sein und bei euch bleiben.
Im Namen des Vaters, des Sohnes und des Heiligen Geistes.
Amen.

56   Gehet hin in Frieden.
Möge Gott euch neue Wege weisen,
Jesus Christus euch begleiten,
und der Heilige Geist euch in eurem Leben stärken.
Amen.

57   Möge der Gott der Liebe, der seine Liebe teilte,
      uns in unserer Liebe für andere bestärken.
Möge der Sohn, der sein Leben teilte,
      uns gnädig sein, damit wir unser Leben mit anderen teilen.
Und möge der Heilige Geist, der in uns wohnt,
      uns befähigen, ausschliesslich
      und immer für andere da zu sein.
Amen.

58   Ewiger Gott,
unser Anfang und unser Ende,
sei unser Ausgang und unser Himmel,
begleite uns auf dem Weg durch den heutigen Tag.
Benütze unsere Hände,
damit wir die Arbeit deiner Schöpfung tun,
und nimm unsere Leben, um anderen neues Leben zu bringen,
das du dieser Welt in Jesus Christus, unserem
Erlöser, gegeben hast.
Amen.

Ordre du culte quotidien

Préparation
Invocation
Psaume ou cantique de louange
Confession des péchés, paroles de pardon

Entrée
Ancien Testament ou lecture des Epîtres
Lecture de l'Evangile
Acclamation
Répons

Affirmation de la foi
Intercessions
Prière du Seigneur

Bénédiction

Cantique

I. Invocation

1
Dieu de grâce et de sainteté,
envoie sur nous aujourd'hui ton Esprit Saint
comme tu l'avais envoyé sur tes apôtres,
le jour de Pentecôte,
afin que nos prières et nos actes
portent témoignage de ce désir qui nous habite:
Nous voulons être un, Seigneur,
afin que le monde croie que nous t'appartenons.
Remplis-nous maintenant de ton amour.

2
O Lumière!
Divine et Sainte Trinité,
Nous qui sommes nés de la terre,
nous ne cessons de te rendre gloire
à l'unisson de la multitude des armées célestes.
Qu'au lever de la lumière du matin,
ta clarté limpide
illumine nos âmes.

3
Feu de l'Esprit:
embrase nos cœurs d'amour pour notre prochain.

Feu de l'Esprit:
éclaire notre sentier et que nous marchions dans la vérité.

Feu de l'Esprit:
lève-toi en nous en une passion pour la liberté.

Feu de l'Esprit:
rassemble-nous pour célébrer ta vie.

4
O Roi céleste, Consolateur, Esprit de vérité,
Tu es présent en tous lieux, et tu remplis toutes choses;
Source de toutes grâces et Dispensateur de vie:
Viens et demeure en nous, purifie-nous de toute impureté
et, dans ta bonté, sauve nos âmes.

5   O Dieu, Esprit Saint,
       viens à nous et au milieu de nous :
       tel un souffle de vent, viens et purifie-nous ;
       telle une flamme, viens et consume-nous ;
       telle une rosée, viens et rafraîchis-nous :
       convaincs, convertis et consacre
       des cœurs et des vies en grand nombre
       pour notre grand bien
       et ta plus grande gloire,
       nous t'en prions au nom de Jésus-Christ.

6   Viens Esprit Saint,
       enflamme nos cœurs qui s'attendent à toi !

       Consume-nous par ton amour,
       et renouvelle-nous en ta propre vie.

7   Esprit de lumière, que ta sagesse nous éclaire.
       *Esprit de Dieu, viens dans nos cœurs, fais de nous ta nouvelle
       création*

       Esprit de silence, rends-nous conscients de la présence de Dieu.
       (Réponse, voir plus haut)

       Esprit de courage, dissipe la crainte en nos cœurs.
       (Réponse, voir plus haut)

       Esprit de feu, embrase-nous de l'amour de Christ.
       (Réponse, voir plus haut)

       Esprit de paix, calme notre esprit pour écouter la Parole de Dieu.
       (Réponse, voir plus haut)

       Esprit de joie, suscite en nous le besoin de proclamer la bonne nouvelle.
       (Réponse, voir plus haut)

       Esprit d'amour, rends-nous sensibles aux besoins des autres.
       (Réponse, voir plus haut)

       Esprit de puissance, accorde-nous toute ton aide et ta force.
       (Réponse, voir plus haut)
       Esprit de vérité, dirige-nous tous dans le chemin du Christ.
       (Réponse, voir plus haut)

8   Sœurs et frères, debout, élevez le cœur
Debout, élevez le regard
Debout, élevez la voix !

Le Dieu vivant,
l'Esprit vivant et agissant de Dieu
nous a rassemblés
pour un témoignage,
pour une célébration,
pour un combat.

Tournez-vous les uns vers les autres,
car Dieu se tourne vers nous !
Adorons notre Dieu !

9   Joie au ciel ! Exulte la terre !
Les masses de la mer mugissent,
la campagne tout entière est en fête.
Les arbres des forêts dansent de joie
devant la face du Seigneur, car il vient,
il vient pour juger la terre.
Il jugera le monde avec justice,
et les peuples selon sa vérité.

(silence)

Les œuvres du Seigneur nous entourent,
Nous répondons par la louange.

L'amour de Dieu s'est manifesté,
Nous répondons par notre foi.

La parole de Dieu nous appelle,
Nous répondons par notre espérance.

Souffle le vent de l'Esprit,
Nous répondons dans la joie.

7.
A mother's love / Mutterliebe
Amour maternel / El amor de una madre

8.
Worship in Spirit / Der Geist bewegt den Gottesdienst
Célébration dans l'Esprit / Celebración en el Espíritu

10   Prions pour que l'eau des rivières soit abondante,
     afin que Christ, notre Seigneur,
     la bénisse et l'amène à son meilleur niveau ;
     qu'il accroisse généreusement le rendement
     de toutes les terres nourricières ;
     qu'il subvienne aux besoins des créatures humaines ;
     qu'il épargne les troupeaux ;
     Et qu'il pardonne nos péchés.
     Seigneur, prends pitié.

     Prions pour les arbres, la végétation,
     la terre cultivée cette année,
     afin que Christ, notre Seigneur, les bénisse ;
     qu'il les fasse prospérer et produire une abondante récolte ;
     qu'il prenne compassion de sa création tout entière,
     et qu'il pardonne nos péchés.
     Seigneur, prends pitié.

     Accrois les ressources de la terre, ô Seigneur ;
     arrose-la abondamment
     et dispose de nous selon ton bon plaisir.
     Couronne de tes faveurs l'année en cours,
     pour le bien des déshérités de ton peuple,
     la veuve, l'orphelin et l'étranger,
     et notre bien à tous.
     Car nos yeux sont sur toi, l'espérance de nos vies,
     pour sanctifier ton saint nom.
     Tu assures notre pain au moment voulu.
     Traite-nous, ô Seigneur, selon ta bonté,
     toi qui assures la nourriture de tous.
     Remplis nos cœurs de joie et de reconnaissance
     afin que, pourvus du nécessaire,
     nous croissions en toute bonne œuvre.
     Amen.

II. Invitation à la prière

11   Au Seigneur la terre et sa plénitude,
     le monde et ceux qui l'habitent.

     Qu'il est bon, qu'il est doux
     de vivre ensemble dans l'unité.

L'amour et la foi se rejoignent,
la justice et la paix se donnent la main.

Si les disciples du Seigneur se taisent,
les pierres que voici crieront.

Seigneur, ouvre nos lèvres
et notre bouche publiera ta louange.

12   Réjouis-toi, peuple du Seigneur !
Célèbre-le pour la vie qui est en toi
et pour Christ qui est au milieu de toi !

Les yeux de tous s'ouvriront !
Le présent prendra un nouveau sens
et l'avenir s'éclairera d'une lumineuse espérance.

Réjouis-toi, peuple du Seigneur !
Courbe la tête devant Celui
qui est ta sagesse et ta force.

Nous nous plaçons devant notre Dieu,
afin qu'il nous touche et nous purifie
par la puissance de Son Esprit.

13   Dans le mystère et la grandeur
la face de Dieu se dévoile,
dans la lumière et le quotidien
l'amour de Christ se révèle.

Face aux forces des hauteurs et à celles des profondeurs
dans la vie et la mort :
l'esprit du Seigneur
se meut au milieu de nous.

Louons le Seigneur.

14
J'allumerai un flambeau
au nom du Seigneur Dieu
lui qui éclaire le monde
et qui a insufflé sa vie en moi.

J'allumerai un flambeau
au nom du divin Fils
il a sauvé le monde
et tendu sa main vers moi.

J'allumerai un flambeau
au nom de l'Esprit divin
qui enveloppe le monde entier
et enrichit mon âme d'aspirations nouvelles.

Allumons trois lumières
en hommage à la trinité de l'amour

Dieu au-dessus de nous,
Dieu à côté de nous,
Dieu au-dessous de nous :
le commencement
et la fin,
le Seigneur éternel.

15
Sœurs et frères
nous voici rassemblés
pour adorer Dieu qui nous offre la liberté
par Jésus-Christ, notre Seigneur.
Car l'esprit de vie en Jésus-Christ
nous a libérés du péché et de la mort.
Car nous n'avons pas reçu un esprit de servitude
pour retomber dans la crainte
mais un esprit d'adoption filiale
qui atteste que nous sommes enfants de Dieu.

16
Nous adorons respectueusement
la Personne impénétrable, Dieu le Père,
la Personne secourable, Dieu le Fils,
la Personne qui témoigne, Dieu le Saint-Esprit.
Nous adorons la Trinité sainte,
trois en un.

III. Louange et adoration

17   Jésus, comme une mère rassemble ses enfants autour d'elle,
Tu es bon envers nous, telle une mère avec ses enfants.

Tu pleures souvent sur nos péchés et notre arrogance,
Avec tendresse, tu nous éloignes de la haine et du jugement.

Tu nous consoles dans notre chagrin et tu panses nos plaies;
Tu nous soignes quand nous sommes malades, d'un lait pur tu nous nourris.

Jésus, par ta mort, nous naissons à une vie nouvelle,
Par ton angoisse et ta peine, nous renaissons à la joie.

C'est par ta tendre bonté que le désespoir se change en confiance;
Par ta clémence, tu nous réconfortes dans nos craintes.

C'est par ton cœur brûlant que les morts revivent:
C'est par un contact avec toi que les pécheurs se redressent.

Seigneur Jésus, guéris-nous dans ta miséricorde:
Dans ton amour et ta tendresse, renouvelle-nous.

Dans ta compassion, transmets-nous grâce et pardon:
Qu'à la beauté du ciel, ton amour nous prépare.

Un cantique de St Anselme

18   Avant que le monde soit
et après la fin de l'éternité,
Tu es Dieu.

Dès la naissance de l'océan
et jusqu'au terme de la course du vent,
Tu es Dieu.

Dans la durée des choses créées
comme dans leur inconstance,
Tu es Dieu.

Dans l'immensité de l'univers
et dans le secret oublié de notre cœur,
Tu es Dieu,
Tu es notre Dieu,
et nous te bénissons.

19   Gloire à toi tout-puissant Seigneur !
Tu as parlé, et des ténèbres a jailli la lumière,
l'ordre succéda au chaos.

(Femmes :)
Tu insufflas dans la glaise du sol une haleine de vie,
et tu nous créas à ton image.

(Hommes :)
Tu regardas l'ouvrage de tes mains,
et tu vis que tout cela était bon.

Tu ne cesses jamais de nous parler, de nous animer, de te soucier de nous.
Nous te louons, Seigneur !

Gloire à toi, Jésus-Christ !
Tel un réfugié, tel un enfant menacé,
Tu es venu à notre rencontre ;
La parole a été faite chair, elle est née dans un lieu oublié.

(Femmes :)
Tu nous as appelés par notre nom, afin de quitter la facilité,
afin d'être tes disciples, tes compagnons de route, tes amis.

(Hommes :)
Tu nous as sauvés en te courbant à nos pieds,
Tu étendis tes bras afin d'emporter nos péchés,
Tu goûtas à la mort pour nous ramener à la vie.

Tu ne cesses jamais de venir à nous, de nous appeler et de nous sauver.
Nous te louons, Seigneur !

Gloire à toi Esprit saint !
Tu as veillé sur le chaos
pour faire naître et pour former la nouvelle création de Dieu.

(Femmes :)
Tu inspiras les prophètes et les évangélistes
afin de trouver la parole à dire en temps opportun.

(Hommes :)
Tu libéras la première Eglise en vue de sa mission
afin qu'elle revendique toute vie pour le maître de Tout.

Tu ne cesses de veiller sur nous, de nous inspirer et de nous libérer.
Nous te louons, Seigneur !

Gloire à Toi, Seigneur Dieu, trois en un !
Tu es au ciel, entouré du chant de tes saints,
et tu es présent, avec nous, maintenant.
Nous t'adorons, Seigneur !

20

J'ai vu l'eau sortir de dessous le seuil du temple :
Là où pénètre le torrent, tout reviendra à la vie.

Sur les deux rives du torrent croissent des arbres fruitiers
produisant des fruits de tous genres :
Leur feuillage ne se flétrit pas, leurs fruits ne manquent pas.

Leurs fruits serviront à nourrir, et leur feuillage, à guérir les nations :
car le torrent d'eau vive
jaillit du trône de Dieu et de l'Agneau.

IV. Confession des péchés

21

Seigneur, tes chemins ne sont pas nos chemins :
tes pensées ne sont pas nos pensées :
ce qui nous paraît comme l'éternité
n'est qu'un court moment pour toi.

Qu'en face de l'éternité
tu nous aides à rester humble.

Traditional Urdu   R.F. Liberius: Pakistan

1. Khu- da - ya, ra - hem kar. Khu- da - ya, ra - hem,
   Have mer - cy on us, Lord, have mer - cy on us.

Khu- da - ya, ra - hem kar. Khu- da - ya, ra - hem.
Have mer - cy on us, Lord, have mer - cy on us.

Khu — da - ya, ra - hem kar, khu - da - ya, ra - hem.
Have mer - cy on us, Lord, have mer - cy on us.

Kyrie eleison. Herr, erbarme dich. Seigneur, aie pitié de nous. Señor, ten piedad de nosotros.
Christe eleison. Christe, erbarme dich. O Christ, aie pitié de nous. Christo, ten piedad de nosotros.

Si nos voix ont chanté tes louanges
mais que la joie est restée absente de nos cœurs ;

Si nous n'avons prié que pour ce qui est possible
et espéré que pour ce qui était visible ;

Si nous avons pris ta grâce comme allant de soi et
estimé que nos demandes instantes devaient être suivies de
réponses immédiates ;

Si d'être aux ordres de l'Esprit est devenu un oreiller de paresse
et si l'attente du Royaume s'est muée en nonchalance ;

S'il nous arrive de croire que nous sommes seuls à compter sur toi
sans jamais considérer combien Toi, Seigneur, tu comptes sur nous :

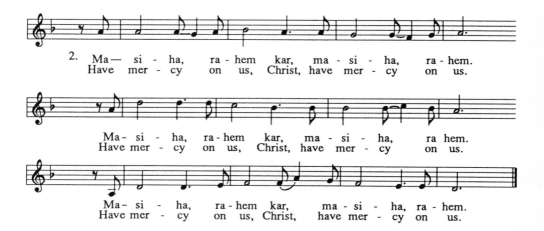

2. Ma — si - ha, ra - hem kar, ma - si - ha, ra - hem.
Have mer - cy on us, Christ, have mer - cy on us.

Ma - si - ha, ra - hem kar, ma - si - ha, ra hem.
Have mer - cy on us, Christ, have mer - cy on us.

Ma — si - ha, ra - hem kar, ma - si - ha, ra - hem.
Have mer - cy on us, Christ, have mer - cy on us.

Kyrie eleison. Herr, erbarme dich. Seigneur, aie pitié de nous. Señor, ten piedad de nosotros.
Christe eleison. Christe, erbarme dich. O Christ, aie pitié de nous. Christo, ten piedad de nosotros.

Si nous avons prié « Esprit source de vie, garde ta création »
tout en nous laissant séduire par la société de consommation.

Si nous avons prié « Esprit de vérité, libère-nous »
tout en préférant la tyrannie du silence.

Si nous avons prié « Esprit d'unité, réconcilie ton peuple »
sans être solidaires des croyants d'autres confessions ou traditions
de notre voisinage.

Si nous avons prié « Esprit Saint, transforme-nous et sanctifie-nous »
sans nous attendre à un bouleversement de nos vies par l'Esprit :

Traditional Urdu   R.F. Liberius: Pakistan

3. Khu - da - ya,   ra - hem kar.   Khu - da - ya,   ra - hem,
   Have mer - cy   on us, Lord,   have mer - cy   on us.

   Khu - da - ya,   ra - hem kar. Khu - da - ya,   ra - hem.
   Have mer - cy   on us,   Lord, have mer - cy   on us.

   Khu — da - ya,   ra - hem   kar,   khu - da - ya,   ra - hem.
   Have   mer - cy on us,   Lord,   have mer - cy   on us.

Kyrie eleison. Herr, erbarme dich. Seigneur, aie pitié de nous. Señor, ten piedad de nosotros.
Christe eleison. Christe, erbarme dich. O Christ, aie pitié de nous. Christo, ten piedad de nosotros.

Ecoute, car c'est ici, de Dieu, la parole véritable :
Heureux tous ceux qui espèrent en Dieu,
Car le Seigneur est miséricordieux et son amour est ferme et inébranlable.
Amen.

22   Esprit de joie,
c'est par toi que Christ vit en nous
et nous en lui :
Pardonne quand nous t'oublions
et omettons de vivre de ta joie.
Esprit de Dieu, pardonne-nous
et conduis-nous à vivre en toi.

Esprit d'amour,
tu nous lies, par amour, à toi-même
et à ceux qui nous entourent
dans le mariage, la famille et la communauté des amis.
Pardonne quand nous faisons tort à ceux que nous aimons
et nous détournons de l'amour de nos amis.
Esprit de Dieu, pardonne-nous
et conduis-nous à vivre en toi.

Esprit du Corps de Christ,
tu nous unis dans l'Eglise
par ta grâce vivifiante et le don d'espérance.
Pardonne quand nous morcelons ton Eglise
et manquons de mettre en œuvre ton amour dans le monde.
Esprit de Dieu, pardonne-nous
et conduis-nous à vivre en toi.

Esprit présent au monde,
qui réconforte et nous rapproche plus près
les uns des autres.
Pardonne nos conflits et nos haines réciproques,
et nos échecs répétés à te reconnaître parmi nous
unique vie de notre vie à tous.
Esprit de Dieu, pardonne-nous
et conduis-nous à vivre en toi.

Comme la colombe se pose en douceur sur l'arbre,
recevez le don de la paix.
Comme le feu brûle librement, éclaire et réchauffe,
recevez le don de la vie.
Comme le vent se meut et danse autour de la terre,
recevez le don précieux de l'Esprit.
Amen.

23   Seigneur Jésus-Christ.
Fils du Dieu vivant,
Prends pitié de moi,
pécheur.

24   Toi qui nous as arrachés à la mort,
nous te rendons grâces!
Accorde-nous le pain de vie,
nous t'en prions!

Toi qui as transformé nos vies,
nous te rendons grâces!
Garde-nous fidèles à jamais,
nous t'en prions!

Toi qui as commencé en nous l'œuvre de la grâce,
nous te rendons grâces!
Achève en nous ton œuvre de salut,
nous t'en prions!

Toi qui as fait de nous ton peuple,
nous te rendons grâces!
Garde-nous tous dans l'unité,
nous t'en prions!

25   Par la foi
présentons-nous devant le Dieu saint
et prenons conscience de ce que nous sommes:
(prière silencieuse)

Nous sommes le peuple des Nouveaux Cieux
et de la Nouvelle Terre,
mais nous sommes loin de combler cet espoir.

Nous sommes le peuple auquel la grâce de
Dieu est donnée,
mais nous sommes loin de la partager avec les autres.

Demandez et vous recevrez,
cherchez et vous trouverez,
frappez, et la vie
s'ouvrira devant vous.
Levez-vous et vivez
dans la liberté et la foi.
Amen.

26   Esprit Saint, défenseur et consolateur,
En toi nous célébrons la présence libératrice du Christ vivant.
Tu souffles où tu veux, tu restaures, tu renouvelles et tu inspires :
Tel le feu, tu purifies.

Esprit Saint, défenseur et consolateur,
Tu exposes au grand jour le mal dans le monde.
Tu prouves le monde coupable en fait de péché.
Tel le feu, tu purifies.

Purifie-nous, mène-nous par delà nos intérêts particuliers.
Soutiens, préserve et prends soin de ta création ;
Nourris, maintiens et dirige tes créatures.
Esprit Saint, défenseur et consolateur,
Tel le feu, tu purifies ;
purifie-nous, nous t'en prions.

27   Confessons
les péchés secrets dissimulés dans les espaces cachés de nos vies
et qui nous tiennent ligotés par inquiétude et par peur,
nous tiennent éloignés de Dieu et nous séparent les uns des autres.

(silence)

Korean   Jacques Berthier: Taizé France

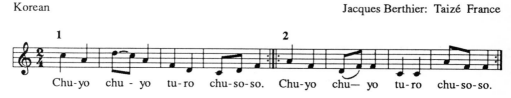

Chu-yo   chu - yo   tu-ro   chu-so-so.   Chu-yo   chu— yo   tu-ro   chu-so-so.

Lord hear us. Höre uns, Gott. Ecoute nous, Dieu. Seigneur, aie pitié. Señor, escúchanos.

Confessons
les paroles de jugement dissimulées dans nos communautés,
les compromis auxquels nous consentons et qui multiplient le mal
jusqu'à produire des moissons de destruction et de mort.

(silence)

Korean

Jacques Berthier: Taizé France

Chu-yo   chu - yo   tu-ro   chu-so-so.   Chu-yo   chu— yo   tu-ro   chu-so-so.

Lord hear us. Höre uns, Gott. Ecoute nous, Dieu. Seigneur, aie pitié. Señor, escúchanos.

Confessons
la satisfaction de soi tout en continuant à vivre désunis,
la facilité avec laquelle nous gardons nos préjugés,
refusant ainsi d'être le peuple de Dieu, uni, pour lequel Jésus a intercédé.

(silence)…

Répons

Dieu, devant lequel rien n'est caché
et qui connaît les motifs de nos cœurs,
c'est lui qui pardonne nos péchés
et qui annonce l'heureuse nouvelle
qui fait de nous un peuple libéré.

V. Recueillement

28
    Esprit de vérité et de bon sens,
    seul capable d'exorciser
    les pouvoirs qui enserrent notre monde
    à un point aussi critique:
    Donne-nous la capacité de discerner
    et de dénoncer le mal,
    afin que nous empruntions les voies qui mènent à la paix,
    par Jésus-Christ.
    Amen.

29
    O Dieu, tu déranges les satisfaits d'eux-mêmes
    Car ton verbe est chargé de force,
    et ta parole s'accomplit.
    Sachions-nous ne pas être satisfaits de nous-mêmes
    tant que la vérité est dévoyée.

Rends nos cœurs attentifs
à ta voix libératrice,
en Jésus-Christ.
Amen.

30   Dieu tout-puissant, ta parole créatrice
a permis que l'eau soit pleine de toutes sortes
d'êtres vivants
et que l'air soit rempli d'oiseaux.
Avec tous les habitants des petites îles du globe,
nous nous réjouissons de la richesse de ta création.
Et nous te prions de donner ta sagesse
à tous les habitants de cette terre,
afin qu'ils la gèrent avec discernement et ne ruinent pas ce que tu as fait vivre
pour nous et nos descendants.
Au nom de Jésus nous t'en prions.
Amen.

31   O Dieu notre créateur,
qui donna à tous
ce que nous sommes et ce que nous avons:
Délie-nous de tout attachement exclusif à nous-mêmes.
Rends-nous aptes à partager
ce que nous sommes,
ce que nous savons,
ce que nous avons
les uns avec les autres,
[dans cette assemblée et] avec le monde que tu aimes.
Au nom du Christ
qui rend ce partage possible.
Amen.

32   Esprit de force et de changement,
Toi dont Jésus fut revêtu
pour devenir l'espoir des nations;
sois aussi déversé sur nous,
sans aucune réserve ni distinction,
afin qu'avec confiance et résolution
nous plantions ta justice sur la terre,
par Jésus-Christ,
Amen.

VI. Confession de foi

33
Nous croyons en un seul Dieu,
le Père, le Tout-puissant,
Créateur du ciel et de la terre,
de toutes les choses visibles et invisibles.

Nous croyons en un seul Seigneur, Jésus-Christ,
le Fils unique de Dieu,
engendré du Père avant tous les siècles,
Lumière venue de la Lumière,
vrai Dieu venu du vrai Dieu,
engendré, non pas créé,
consubstantiel au Père ;
par lui tout a été fait.
Pour nous et pour notre salut il descendit des cieux ;
par le Saint-Esprit il a pris chair
de la Vierge Marie
et il s'est fait homme.
Il a été crucifié pour nous sous Ponce Pilate,
il a souffert, il a été enseveli,
il est ressuscité le troisième jour selon les Ecritures,
il est monté aux cieux.

Il siège à la droite du Père
et il reviendra dans la gloire
juger les vivants et les morts ;
son règne n'aura pas de fin.

Nous croyons en l'Esprit Saint,
qui est Seigneur et donne la vie,
qui procède du Père ;
qui avec le Père et le Fils
est adoré et glorifié,
qui a parlé par les Prophètes.
Nous croyons l'Eglise une, sainte, catholique et apostolique.
Nous confessons un seul baptême pour le pardon des péchés.
Nous attendons la résurrection des morts
et la vie du monde à venir.
Amen.

Symbole de Nicée

34
        Je crois en Dieu,
        le Père tout-puissant,
        Créateur du ciel et de la terre.

        Je crois en Jésus-Christ,
        son Fils unique,
        notre Seigneur,
        qui a été conçu du Saint-Esprit
        et qui est né de la Vierge Marie ;
        il a souffert sous Ponce-Pilate,
        il a été crucifié, il est mort,
        il a été enseveli,
        il est descendu au séjour des morts ;
        le troisième jour, il est ressuscité des morts ;
        il est monté aux cieux ;
        il siège à la droite de Dieu,
        le Père tout-puissant,
        d'où il viendra
        juger les vivants et les morts.

        Je crois en l'Esprit Saint,
        la sainte Eglise catholique,
        la communion des saints,
        la rémission des péchés,
        la résurrection de la chair
        et la vie éternelle.
        Amen.

                        Symbole des Apôtres

VII. Intercession

35
        O Dieu notre Père,
        délivre nos rivages des armements de mort,
        nos territoires de tout ce qui prive nos jeunes gens d'amour et de liberté.
        Que les flots [de l'océan Pacifique]
        portent partout des messages de paix et de bonne volonté.
        Rejette du milieu de nous toutes les coutumes cruelles et brutales.
        Que nos enfants se baignent sans crainte
        et respirent un air pur tout rempli de l'Esprit Saint.

O Seigneur Jésus,
bénis chaque artisan de cette paix intérieure
qui abat les murs de haine ;
et unis-nous par les bras étendus de ta croix,
afin que tous les peuples de la terre vivent ensemble avec bonheur.
Amen.

36   O Dieu,
toi qui donnes la vie,
nous te prions pour l'Eglise dans le monde entier.
Sanctifie sa vie, renouvelle son culte ;
donne puissance à son témoignage,
rétablis son unité,
donne force à ceux qui recherchent ensemble
l'obéissance qui nous unira.
Guéris les divisions qui séparent tes enfants
les uns des autres,
afin qu'ils gardent l'unité de l'esprit
par le lien de la paix.
Amen.

37   O Dieu,
qui aime la justice et établis la paix sur la terre,
nous t'apportons la désunion de notre monde aujourd'hui ;
la violence absurde et les guerres qui brisent le courage des peuples ;
le militarisme et la course aux armements qui menacent la vie de la terre ;
la cupidité humaine et l'injustice qui engendrent la haine et le conflit.
Envoie ton Esprit et renouvelle la face de la terre :
Enseigne-nous la compassion à l'égard de toute la famille humaine ;
affermis la volonté de tous ceux qui luttent pour la paix et la justice ;
conduis les nations sur les sentiers de la paix,
et donne-nous cette paix que le monde ne peut pas donner.
Amen.

38   Seigneur, par le sang de tes martyrs,
rassemble dans la joie tous les enfants dispersés de ton Eglise ;
et tous ceux qui pleurent avec amertume sur sa triste désunion.
C'est Toi qui dispenses la grâce de ton Salut.

39   Intercédons pour la venue du Royaume.

O Dieu, dans la douleur de ceux que l'on torture,
insuffle la paix;

dans le tourment des affamés
insuffle du rassasiement;

dans les plaies de notre planète,
insuffle du bien-être;

dans la mort de tes créatures,
insuffle la vie;

dans le cœur de quiconque espère en toi,
insuffle ta propre vie.

Que vienne ton règne,
que soit faite ta volonté,
car c'est à toi qu'appartiennent le règne, la puissance et la gloire,
maintenant et à jamais.

Notre Dieu est avec nous.

Nous célébrons le miracle de vivre et d'être !
Nous célébrons le miracle de la création !
Que Dieu nous aime,
nos vies sont un bienfait de Dieu,
avec joie, rendons grâces!
Amen.

40   Tandis que nous partageons, en ce jour, la vie de votre Eglise,
nous demandons que notre témoignage soit fidèle à Jésus-Christ.
Donne-nous une voix pour les sans-voix
Nous partageons votre recueillement
où le silence seul rend hommage à la souffrance.

Donne-nous des larmes en face des soucis !
Et des rires de joie tandis que nous expérimentons les
merveilles de ta création:

Donne-nous de la détermination pour dénoncer l'injustice.
Anime-nous, Seigneur, de ton éternelle bonté
envers les désespérés qui croisent notre route:

Donne-nous d'être honnêtes à reconnaître nos perplexités !
Que nos rapports avec le prochain soient loyaux,
car tu nous appelles, Seigneur, à œuvrer avec toi dans une
communion confiante,
que par nos prières notre amour s'unisse à ton amour pour le monde.

Les ressources infinies de l'Espérance sont dans la seule grâce de Dieu.
Amen.

41 Souviens-toi, Seigneur, de la chute des pluies, des eaux et des rivières : bénis-les.

Souviens-toi, Seigneur, des plantes, des semences et des fruits des champs pour l'année : bénis-les et rends-les abondants.

Souviens-toi, Seigneur, de la sécurité de ta sainte église, dans toutes les villes de tous les pays.

Souviens-toi, Seigneur, de protéger l'humanité, les êtres vivants, et moi, ton indigne serviteur.

Souviens-toi, Seigneur, de nos pères et de nos mères, de nos frères et de nos sœurs qui se sont endormis et sont entrés dans le repos.

Souviens-toi, Seigneur, des captifs de ton peuple et ramène-les en paix dans leurs demeures.

Souviens-toi, Seigneur, des affligés et de ceux qui souffrent.

Souviens-toi, Seigneur, de tes serviteurs, les pauvres que l'on opprime : fais-leur miséricorde, maintiens-les dans une foi authentique, que l'Esprit les habite, aidés par notre joie spirituelle et notre amour de tous.
Amen.

42 O Dieu, sois présent parmi nous pour tous les humains de la terre.
Ouvre nos yeux au Salut qui est en toi,
révèle-toi à l'humanité aveuglée.

Fais luire ta face sur ceux qui sont terrassés par la maladie. Donne-leur ton assurance et ta paix.

A tous les pauvres, à tous les faibles sur qui pèse la misère, donne ta connaissance, sois leur soutien. Qu'ils soient comblés en toi.

Accorde aux puissants et aux riches le pouvoir qu'ils n'ont pas. Donne-leur du discernement pour qu'ils soient libres de ta liberté, libres d'aimer.

A nous tous, donne ta paix et ta vie.
Amen.

43   Là où l'ignorance, l'égoïsme et l'indifférence
ont déchiré la vie communautaire,
donne ta lumière, ô Dieu d'amour.

Là où l'injustice et l'oppression
ont brisé le courage des peuples,
donne ta lumière, ô Dieu qui libère.

Là où la faim et la pauvreté, la maladie et la mort
ont fait de l'existence un fardeau insupportable,
donne ta lumière, ô Dieu de grâce.

Là où la méfiance et la haine, les luttes et la guerre
ont remis en question ta bonté,
donne ta lumière, ô Dieu de paix.

Eternel Dieu,
ouvre les yeux des nations et des peuples
afin qu'ils marchent à la lumière de ton amour ;
extirpe des nations et des peuples l'ignorance et l'entêtement,
afin qu'ils s'abreuvent aux sources de ta bonté.
Amen.

44   Viens, Esprit Saint, renouvelle la création tout entière.
Que le vent et le feu
de ta vie créatrice
réveillent ton Eglise en ce jour.
Accorde-nous sagesse et foi,
afin de connaître
la grande espérance à laquelle nous sommes appelés.
Viens, Esprit Saint,
Renouvelle la création tout entière.

Toi qui donne la vie,
veille sur ta création.
Mets-nous en face de notre rapacité
dans l'utilisation de tes biens.
Ne nous laisse pas faire
alors que nous pillons et détruisons.
Suscite partout
de nouvelles initiatives pour la sauvegarde
de tout ce qui vit, respire et
existe quelque part.
Viens, Esprit Saint,
Renouvelle la création tout entière.

Esprit de vérité,
libère-nous
afin d'émerger en tant qu'enfants de Dieu.
Ouvre nos oreilles
afin d'entendre
les plaintes du monde.
Ouvre nos bouches
afin que nous devenions la voix
des sans-voix.
Ouvre nos yeux
afin que ta vision de la paix et de la justice
devienne aussi la nôtre.
Anime-nous de ta vérité prophétique
qui nous donnera courage et foi.
Viens, Esprit Saint,
Renouvelle la création tout entière.

Esprit d'unité,
réconcilie ton peuple.
Donne-nous la sagesse
de ne maintenir que ce qui est
nécessaire pour être ton Eglise.
Fais-nous la grâce
de renoncer
à ces choses
dont tu peux te dispenser.
Donne-nous à voir ta grandeur
afin que notre étroitesse de cœur
soit remise en question
et que nous nous réunissions
dans l'humilité qui convient.
Viens, Esprit Saint,
Renouvelle la création tout entière.

Esprit Saint,
transforme et sanctifie-nous
à l'heure où nous assumons cette tâche
en ton nom.
Enrichis-nous des dons qui nous sont nécessaires,
afin d'être ton Eglise,
en esprit et en vérité.
Viens, Esprit Saint,
Renouvelle la création tout entière.

45   O Seigneur tout-puissant,
tu guéris nos âmes et nos corps;
c'est toi qui abaisses et qui exaltes,
qui frappes et qui bandes nos plaies.
Dans ta grande miséricorde visite, en ce jour,
nos frères et nos sœurs malades.
Etends ta main sur eux,
cette main qui donne santé et guérison,
relève-les de leur lit de maladie
et qu'ils se rétablissent.

Chasse tout esprit de maladie,
enlève toute douleur et toute fièvre;
et s'ils ont commis des fautes et des transgressions,
remets-leur leurs péchés et pardonne-leur.
Seigneur notre Dieu,
tu es miséricordieux envers ta création entière,
et tu aimes toutes tes créatures.
Par la compassion de ton Fils premier-né,
et par ton Esprit saint, bon et vivifiant,
sois béni, dès maintenant et à jamais,
dans les siècles des siècles.
Amen.

46 Souviens-toi, Seigneur, de cette ville où nous habitons,
de toute ville et de toute contrée, et de ceux qui y vivent dans la foi.

Romania

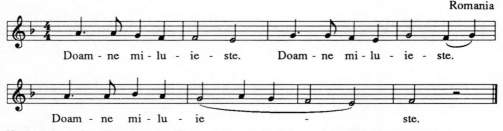

Doam - ne mi - lu - ie - ste.   Doam - ne mi - lu - ie - ste.

Doam - ne mi - lu - ie   -   ste.

Kyrie eleison. Lord have mercy. Herr, erbarme dich. Seigneur, aie pitié. Señor, ten piedad.

Souviens-toi, Seigneur, de ceux qui sont en mer, des voyageurs, des
malades, des prisonniers, de tous ceux qui peinent et de leur Salut.

Répons

Souviens-toi, Seigneur, de ceux qui apportent des dons et font le bien dans
tes saintes Eglises, de ceux qui pensent aux pauvres.

Répons

Et accorde-nous à tous tes miséricordes, et donne-nous de glorifier et de
changer d'une seule voix et d'un seul cœur ton Nom vénérable et magnifi-
que, Père, Fils et Saint-Esprit, maintenant et toujours et dans les siècles des
siècles.

Répons

Que les miséricordes de notre grand Dieu et Sauveur Jésus-Christ soient avec
nous tous.
Amen.

47 Prions ensemble.

Parce que le monde est beau
et que la beauté est une chose fragile
et que nous sommes les gérants de la création,
nous avons besoin de toi, Seigneur,
Besoin de Toi, ô Dieu.

Parce que le savoir paraît illimité
et que nous ne savons pas ce qui est au-delà de notre savoir,
nous avons besoin de toi, Seigneur,
Besoin de Toi, ô Dieu.

Parce qu'il nous est possible de vivre sans toi,
que nous sommes libres de nous opposer à toi,
et que nous pourrions idolâtrer notre propre bon sens,
nous avons besoin de toi, Seigneur,
Besoin de Toi, ô Dieu.

Parce que tu vins parmi nous,
que tu t'assis à nos côtés
et tu nous entendis parler tout en t'ignorant,
que tu as guéri nos douleurs et nous a permis de te blesser,
puisque tu nous aimas jusqu'à la fin
et triomphas de toutes nos haines,
nous avons besoin de toi, Seigneur,
Besoin de Toi, ô Dieu.
Amen.

48   Seigneur, Dieu de la vie, nous te rendons grâces de nous avoir libérés du
pouvoir du péché et de la mort. Sois remercié pour ces gens pleins de bonne
volonté et de courage, qui luttent en plein milieu des peines du monde, afin
d'y faire briller ta lumière.
Esprit de vérité, viens et libère-nous.

Seigneur, Dieu de la vie, par ta grâce, Jésus-Christ a éclairé nos vies, ainsi
que le monde entier, de ta lumière. Illumine nos cœurs afin que nous
débordions d'espérance. Sois remercié de nous donner des guides qui voient
loin et à l'esprit créatif pour nous entraîner vers plus de vie et d'espoir.
Esprit de vérité, viens et libère-nous.

Seigneur, Dieu de la vie, nous te sommes reconnaissants de la multitude
d'hommes et de femmes de conviction qui, au cours de l'histoire, ont
répondu à ton appel d'espérance et de liberté. Ouvre nos yeux et sensibilise
nos oreilles, afin de te voir à l'œuvre, et d'entendre l'écho de tes hauts faits
dans le monde et dans nos vies. Fais tomber les barrières qui emprisonnent et
divisent les peuples ; et affranchis-les pour une vie riche et heureuse.
Esprit de vérité, viens et libère-nous

49   Esprit de paix, remplis toute la création de ta présence transformatrice. Que
les dirigeants de tous les pays gouvernent avec sagesse et justice. Que toutes
les nations jouissent de la tranquillité, et que leurs filles et leurs fils soient
bénis. Que les êtres humains, les animaux et la nature prospèrent et soient
épargnés par la maladie. Que les champs produisent du fruit en abondance et
que la terre soit fertile. Que la face de tous ceux qui sont ennemis se tourne
vers la paix.

From "Missa da Terra Sem Males"   D. Pedro Casaldáliga, Pedro Tierra, Martin Coplas:
                                                         Guarany, Brazil--Paraguay

Sha - lom,   sa - wi - di,   a paz.   Sha-lom,   sa - wi - di,   a paz.

Peace Friede Paix Paz

Esprit d'unité, nous prions pour ton Eglise. Emplis-la de vérité et de paix. Là où elle est corrompue, purifie-la ; là où elle est dans l'erreur, conduis-la vers la vérité ; là où elle est plongée dans la confusion, réforme-la ; là où elle est dans la vérité, affermis-la ; là où elle est dans le besoin, soulage-la ; là où elle est divisée, réunis-la.

Répons

Esprit d'amour, garde ceux qui veillent et qui pleurent, et confie à tes anges ceux qui dorment. Soigne les malades, donne le repos à ceux qui sont accablés, et du courage aux femmes en train d'enfanter, apaise ceux qui souffrent et bénis les mourants.

Répons

50   En un monde où les images de guerre dominent
            Libère-nous, Seigneur, de la tyrannie des antagonismes.

            En un monde rempli de barrières
            Délivre-nous de la tyrannie raciale.

            Nous qui jadis n'étions pas un peuple,
            Fais de nous ton peuple, une communauté vivante,
            n'ayant qu'un cœur et qu'une âme,
            mettant tout en commun.

VIII. Bénédiction

51   Prions :
            Jésus-Christ, notre Seigneur,
            parce que tu rompis le pain avec les pauvres
            que tu fus regardé avec mépris.

            Parce que tu as rompu le pain avec les pécheurs et les parias
            que tu fus considéré comme un impie.

Parce que tu rompis le pain avec des gens en fête
que tu fus traité d'ivrogne et de glouton.

Parce que tu rompis le pain dans la chambre haute
que tu scellas ainsi ta volonté de suivre le chemin qui te mena à la croix.

Parce que tu rompis le pain sur le chemin d'Emmaüs
que tu fis tomber les écailles des yeux des disciples.
Parce que tu rompis le pain et le partageas,
nous allons le faire aussi,
et te prions de le bénir.

Jésus-Christ, notre Seigneur,
mets ta bénédiction sur le pain que nous rompons
et sur notre communion les uns avec les autres.
Renouvelle notre vie en commun
afin qu'ensemble nous partagions les Ecritures,
et que nos cœurs brûlent au-dedans de nous tandis que nous sommes en
chemin.
Amen.

52   Allez avec la force que vous avez
       Allez simplement
            gaiement
            aimablement
       toujours soucieux d'aimer
       et l'Esprit sera avec vous.

53   Dieu tout-puissant:
       que la hardiesse de ton Esprit nous transforme,
       que la bonté de ton Esprit nous dirige,
       que les dons de ton Esprit nous dotent des qualités
       qui nous permettent de te servir et de t'adorer,
       dès maintenant et à jamais.
       Par Jésus-Christ notre Seigneur.
       Amen.

54   Seigneur bien-aimé, aide-nous à tenir bon sans tension,
       à persévérer même sans réussir,
       à aboutir sans effort exagéré,
       afin qu'en tout ce que nous faisons
       la gloire n'en revienne qu'à Toi.
       Amen.

55

Que le Dieu tout-puissant te bénisse !
Que les bénédictions des cieux d'en haut,
les bénédictions de l'abîme étendu sous terre,
les bénédictions des mammelles et du sein,
les bénédictions des graines et des fleurs,
les bénédictions des montagnes antiques,
aux frontières des collines d'antan,
soient avec vous et vous accompagnent.
Au nom du Père et du Fils et du Saint-Esprit.
Amen.

56

Allez en paix.
Puisse le Dieu Saint vous surprendre.
en chemin,
Christ Jésus être votre compagnon de route,
et le Saint Esprit rendre légère votre démarche.
Amen.

57

Que le Dieu d'amour qui a partagé son amour avec nous,
    renforce notre amour pour les autres.
Que le Fils qui fit don de sa vie
    nous fasse la grâce de partager notre vie avec les autres.
Et que l'Esprit Saint, demeurant en nous,
    nous accorde pouvoir et force
    d'être toujours là pour les autres.
Amen.

58

Eternel Dieu,
notre commencement et notre fin,
sois notre point de départ et notre destination
et accompagne-nous durant le trajet de ce jour.
Que nos mains
servent à l'œuvre de ta création ;
que nos vies contribuent à transmettre aux autres
la vie nouvelle que tu donnes à ce monde,
par Jésus Christ, le Sauveur de tous.
Amen.

Orden de culto diario

Preparación
Invocación
Salmo o cántico de alabanza
Confesión de pecados, palabras de absolución

Introducción de la Palabra
Antiguo Testamento o lectura de las Epístolas
Lectura del Evangelio
Aclamación
Respuesta a la Palabra

Afirmación de fe
Intercesiones
Oración del Señor

Bendición

Himno

I. Invocaciones

1
Dios de gracia y de santidad,
derrama sobre nosotros en este día tu Santo Espíritu,
así como lo derramaste sobre tus discípulos
el día de Pentecostés,
para que nuestras oraciones y acciones
sean testigos de tu presencia entre nosotros
Queremos ser uno, Señor,
para que el mundo crea que somos
tuyos. Llénanos ahora de tu amor.

2
Oh Luz,
divina y única Santa Trinidad,
nosotros, simples mortales,
junto con las huestes celestiales
queremos glorificarte siempre.
Al despuntar el alba
derrama sobre nuestras almas
tu inconfundible luz.

3
Llama del Espíritu:
enciende nuestros corazones de amor por nuestro prójimo.

Llama del Espíritu:
ilumina nuestra senda para caminar en tu verdad.

Llama del Espíritu:
despierta en nosotros pasión por la libertad.

Llama del Espíritu
congréganos en la celebración de tu vida.

4
Rey celestial, Consolador, Espíritu de Verdad
presente en todo lugar y en todas las cosas;
fuente de toda bendición y Dador de Vida:
Ven y habita en nosotros, purifícanos
y en tu bondad, salva nuestras almas.

5   Oh Dios, Espíritu Santo,
ven y habita entre nosotros:
como el viento ven y límpianos;
como el fuego ven y consúmenos;
como el rocío ven y refréscanos:
convence, convierte y consagra
nuestros corazones y vidas
para el bien
y la gloria de tu nombre.
Te lo pedimos por el amor de Jesús.

6   Ven Espíritu Santo,
¡ inflama nuestros corazones que te aguardan !

Consúmenos con tu amor
y renuévanos en tu vida.

7   Espíritu de Luz: Que tu sabiduría nos ilumine.
Espíritu de Dios, ven a nuestros corazones, haznos tu nueva creación.

Espíritu de Solaz: Que seamos conscientes de la presencia de Dios.
(La misma respuesta anterior)

Espíritu de Valentía: Echa fuera de nuestros corazones el temor .
(La misma respuesta anterior)

Espíritu de Fuego: Enciéndenos con el amor de Cristo.
(La misma respuesta anterior)

Espíritu de Paz: Ayúdanos a esperar en ti y a escuchar la voz de Dios.
(La misma respuesta anterior)

Espíritu de Gozo: Inspíranos para proclamar tus buenas nuevas.
(La misma respuesta anterior)

Espíritu de Amor: Haznos sensibles a las necesidades de los otros.
(La misma respuesta anterior)

Espíritu de Poder: Danos tu ayuda y tu fortaleza.
(La misma respuesta anterior)

Espíritu de Verdad: Condúcenos en el camino de Cristo.
(La misma respuesta anterior)

8   Hermanas y hermanos – Levántense
Levántense y eleven sus corazones
Levántense y eleven sus miradas
Levántense y eleven sus voces.

El Dios vivo,
el Espíritu de Dios que vive y se mueve entre nosotros,
nos ha llamado a todos juntos
al testimonio,
a la celebración,
a la lucha.

Extiendan sus brazos unos a otros,
ya que nuestro Dios los extiende hacia nosotros.
¡Adoremos a Dios!

9   Alégrense los cielos, y gócese la tierra;
brame el mar y su plenitud.
Regocíjese el campo, y todo lo que en él está;
entonces todos los árboles del bosque rebosarán de
alegría, delante del Señor ya que Dios viene;
viene a juzgar la tierra.
Juzgará al mundo con justicia,
y a las naciones con su verdad.

(silencio)

La obra de Dios nos rodea.
Respondemos con alabanza.

El amor de Dios es visible.
Respondemos con fe.

La Palabra de Dios nos llama.
Repondemos en esperanza.

El viento del Espíritu sopla.
Respondemos con gozo.

10   Oremos por las aguas de los ríos durante este año,
      que Cristo, nuestro Señor,
      las bendiga y las haga crecer en su medida,
      que dé un toque de alegría a los campos,
      sostenga a los seres humanos,
      guarde el ganado
      y perdone nuestros pecados.
      Señor, ten piedad.

      Oremos por los árboles, la vegetación
      y las plantaciones en este año;
      que Cristo, nuestro Señor, las bediga
      para que crezcan y fructifiquen en abundancia,
      que se compadezca de su creación
      y perdone nuestros pecados.
      Señor, ten piedad.

      Concede, oh Señor, tu bendición a la tierra,
      riégala,
      y dispón de nuestras vidas como lo creas conveniente.
      Colma este año con tus bendiciones,
      por amor de los más pobres de tu pueblo,
      la viuda, el huérfano, el extranjero,
      y por amor de nosotros.
      Nuestros ojos están puestos en ti, esperanza nuestra,
      y buscan tu santo nombre.
      Tú nos das el alimento a su debido tiempo.
      Trátanos, Señor, de acuerdo a tu bondad,
      tú, que alimentas a todos.
      Colma nuestros corazones de gozo y de gracia,
      para que teniendo siempre lo suficiente,
      crezcamos en toda buena obra.
      Amén.

II. Llamados a la adoración

11   El mundo es de Dios,
      la tierra y todo lo que en ella habita.

      Mirad cuán bueno y delicioso es
      habitar juntos en armonía.

El amor y la fe se encuentran
la justicia y la paz se abrazan.

Si los discípulos del Señor se callan
las piedras gritarán.

Señor, abre nuestros labios
para que proclamen alabanza a tu nombre.

12 ¡ Regocíjate, oh pueblo de Dios !
¡ Celebra la vida que hay en ti
y la presencia de Cristo a tu alrededor !

¡ Nuestros ojos serán abiertos !
El presente tendrá nuevo sentido
y el futuro brillará con esperanza.

¡ Regocíjate, oh pueblo de Dios !
Inclínate ante el Unico
que es nuestra sabiduría y fortaleza.

Nos presentamos ante nuestro Dios,
para ser tocados y purificados
por el poder de su Espíritu.

13 En lo majestuoso y misterioso
vemos el rostro de Dios;
en lo terrenal y lo cotidiano
conocemos el amor de Cristo.

En las alturas y en las profundidades,
en la vida y en la muerte:
El Espíritu de Dios
se mueve entre nosotros.

Alabemos al Señor.

14   Encenderé una luz
        en el nombre de Dios
        quien iluminó el mundo
        e insufló en mí su aliento divino.

        Encenderé una luz
        en el nombre del Hijo
        quien salvó al mundo
        y me tendió su mano.

        Encenderé una luz
        en el nombre del Espíritu Santo
        quien envuelve al mundo
        y bendice mi alma con nuevos anhelos.

        Encendamos tres luces
        en honor a la Trinidad de amor;

        Dios de los cielos,
        Dios de la tierra,
        Dios compañero,
        el principio y el fin,
        Dios eterno.

15   Hermanas y hermanos,
        nos hemos reunido
        para adorar a Dios
        quien nos da libertad
        por medio de nuestro Señor Jesucristo.
        Porque el Espíritu de vida en Cristo Jesús
        nos ha liberado de la ley del pecado y de la muerte.
        Porque no hemos recibido el Espíritu de esclavitud
        para vivir en temor
        sino el Espíritu de adopción
        quien da testimonio que somos hijos de Dios.

16   Con reverencia adoramos al misterio en Dios el Padre,
        a la respuesta en Dios el Hijo,
        al testimonio en el Espíritu de Santidad.
        Adoramos a la Santa Trinidad,
        tres personas en una.

III. Alabanzas y adoración

17 Jesús, como una madre tú reúnes a tu pueblo:
Eres tan tierno como una madre con sus hijos.

Sufres con nuestros pecados y orgullo:
Cariñosamente nos apartas del odio y la condenación.

Nos consuelas en la tristeza y sanas nuestras heridas:
En la enfermedad nos cuidas y nos das el mejor alimento.

Jesús, en tu muerte nos das nueva vida:
En tu angustia y dolor renace nuestra alegría.

Tu bondad transforma nuestra desesperanza en confianza:
Con tu ternura desaparecen nuestros temores.

Tu calor infunde vida a lo yerto:
Tu toque transforma a los pecadores en justos.

Señor Jesús, en tu misericordia sánanos:
Con tu amor y ternura transfórmanos.

En tu compasión concédenos gracia y perdón:
Y que tu amor nos prepare para gozar de la vida eterna.

Canción de San Anselmo

18 Antes de que el mundo existiese
y hasta el fin de la eternidad,
tú eres Dios.

Desde la profundidad del océano
hasta el silbido del viento en su vagar,
tú eres Dios.

En la invariabilidad de lo creado
y en su versatilidad,
tú eres Dios.

En la inmensidad del universo
y en el olvidado rincón de nuestros corazones,
tú eres Dios.
Tú eres nuestro Dios
y nosotros te bendecimos.

19

¡ Gloria sea a ti, Dios Todopoderoso !
Tú hablaste, y la luz iluminó la oscuridad
y lo creado surgió del caos.

(Mujeres:)
Tú respiraste en el polvo de la tierra
y nos formaste a tu imagen.

(Hombres:)
Tú miraste la obra de tus manos
y declaraste que todo era bueno.

Y todavía hablas, respiras
y mantienes tus ojos sobre nosotros.
Te alabamos.

¡ Gloria a ti, Jesucristo !
Tú has venido a nuestro encuentro como refugiado, como niño amenazado,
la palabra hecha carne, nacido en un lugar olvidado.

(Mujeres:)
Tú nos llamas, por nombre, a dejar nuestra comodidad
para ser tus discípulas, compañeras y amigas.

(Hombres:)
Para salvarnos te humillaste,
extendiste tus brazos para quitar nuestros pecados
y saboreaste la muerte para traernos la vida.

Y todavía sales a nuestro encuentro, nos llamas y nos salvas.
Te alabamos.

¡ Gloria a ti, Santo Espíritu !
Tú anidaste sobre el caos,
concibiendo y dando forma a la nueva creación de Dios.

(Mujeres:)
Tú inspiraste a profetas y a evangelistas
a descubrir la palabra precisa para el momento oportuno.

(Hombres:)
Tú liberaste a la iglesia primitiva para una misión,
la de proclamar la vida para el Señor de todo.

Y todavía anidas entre nosotros, nos inspiras y liberas.
Te alabamos.

¡ Gloria a tí, Dios Trino y Uno !
Estás rodeado por el canto de los santos en el cielo
y presente aquí y ahora entre nosotros.
Te adoramos.

20   Vi correr agua por los umbrales del templo :
Por donde un río fluye todo vuelve a la vida.

En las riberas del río crecen árboles
cargados de toda clase de fruto :
Sus hojas no se secarán y su fruto no faltará.

Sus frutos servirán de alimento,
sus hojas de medicina para las naciones :
Porque el río de aguas de vida
fluye del trono de Dios y del Cordero.

IV. Confesiones

21   Señor, tus caminos no son nuestros caminos,
tus pensamientos no son nuestros pensamientos :
aquello que nos parece eterno
es sólo un momento para ti.

Al contemplar lo eterno
ayúdanos a ser humildes.

Traditional Urdu   R.F. Liberius: Pakistan

1. Khu-da - ya, ra - hem kar. Khu-da - ya, ra - hem,
Have mer - cy on us, Lord, have mer - cy on us.

Khu-da - ya, ra - hem kar. Khu-da - ya, ra - hem.
Have mer - cy on us, Lord, have mer - cy on us.

Khu— da - ya, ra - hem kar, khu - da - ya, ra - hem.
Have mer - cy on us, Lord, have mer - cy on us.

Kyrie eleison. Herr, erbarme dich. Seigneur, aie pitié de nous. Señor, ten piedad de nosotros.
Christe eleison. Christe, erbarme dich. O Christ, aie pitié de nous. Christo, ten piedad de nosotros.

Si sólo nuestros labios te han cantado alabanzas
y nuestros corazones han estado lejos de ti;

Si solamente hemos orado por lo que era posible
y esperado sólo en lo que era evidente;

Si hemos creído merecer tu gracia
y esperado respuestas inmediatas a nuestras peticiones;

Si hemos permitido que el esperar en tu Espíritu se convierta en pereza
y que la apatía reemplace la esperanza de tu Reino;

Si hemos creído que sólo nosotros esperamos en ti
sin considerar que tú también, Señor, esperas en nosotros:

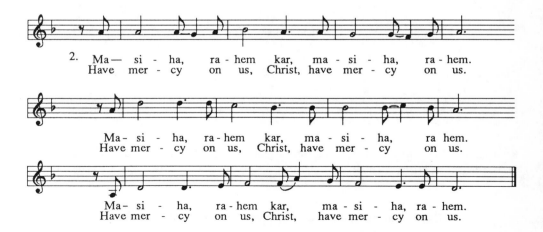

2. Ma— si - ha, ra - hem kar, ma - si - ha, ra - hem.
Have mer - cy on us, Christ, have mer - cy on us.

Ma— si - ha, ra - hem kar, ma - si - ha, ra hem.
Have mer - cy on us, Christ, have mer - cy on us.

Ma— si - ha, ra - hem kar, ma - si - ha, ra - hem.
Have mer - cy on us, Christ, have mer - cy on us.

Kyrie eleison. Herr, erbarme dich. Seigneur, aie pitié de nous. Señor, ten piedad de nosotros.
Christe eleison. Christe, erbarme dich. O Christ, aie pitié de nous. Christo, ten piedad de nosotros.

Si hemos orado « Dador de la vida, mantén tu creación » ;
y hemos sucumbido al consumismo.

Si hemos orado « Espíritu de verdad, libéranos » ;
y luego escogido la esclavitud del silencio.

Si hemos orado « Espíritu de Unidad, reconcilia a tu pueblo » ;
y no nos reunimos en nuestra comunidad
con personas de otras confesiones y tradiciones.

Si hemos orado « Espíritu Santo, transfórmanos y santifícanos »
y no esperamos a que el Espíritu cambiase nuestras vidas :

Traditional Urdu   R.F. Liberius: Pakistan

3. Khu- da - ya,   ra - hem kar.   Khu- da - ya,   ra - hem,
Have mer - cy   on us, Lord,   have mer - cy   on us.

Khu- da - ya,   ra - hem kar. Khu- da - ya,   ra - hem.
Have mer - cy   on us, Lord, have mer - cy   on us.

Khu — da - ya, ra - hem   kar,   khu- da - ya, ra - hem.
Have   mer - cy   on us, Lord,   have mer - cy   on us.

Kyrie eleison. Herr, erbarme dich. Seigneur, aie pitié de nous. Señor, ten piedad de nosotros.
Christe eleison. Christe, erbarme dich. O Christ, aie pitié de nous. Christo, ten piedad de nosotros.

Estemos atentos porque ésta es la verdadera palabra de Dios
bienaventurados todos los que esperan en el Señor,
porque Dios es misericordioso y su amor firme e inquebrantable.
Amén.

22   Espíritu de Gozo
        a través de ti,
        Cristo vive en nosotros y nosotros en El.
        Perdónanos por olvidarte
        y no permanecer en tu gozo.
        Espíritu de Dios, perdónanos
        y condúcenos hacia la vida contigo.

        Espíritu de amor,
        tú nos mantienes unidos a ti
        y a los que nos rodean:
        nuestra pareja, nuestra familia y amigos.
        Perdónanos cuando herimos a nuestros seres queridos
        y cuando despreciamos el amor de nuestros amigos.
        Espíritu de Dios, perdónanos
        y condúcenos hacia la vida contigo.

        Espíritu del cuerpo de Cristo,
        tú nos unes en la Iglesia
        por tu gracia vivificante y el don de la esperanza.
        Perdónanos por fragmentar tu Iglesia
        y por no poner en obra tu amor en el mundo.
        Espíritu de Dios, perdónanos
        y condúcenos hacia la vida contigo.

        Espíritu de Dios presente en el mundo,
        que nos reconfortas y nos unes
        los unos con los otros,
        perdona nuestros conflictos y odios,
        perdónanos por no reconocerte en medio nuestro,
        a ti que vives en todos nosotros.
        Espíritu de Dios, perdónanos
        y condúcenos hacia la vida contigo.

        Como la paloma que se posa suavemente sobre el árbol,
        recibe el espíritu de paz.
        Como la llama que se eleva dando luz y calor,
        recibe el don de la vida.
        Como el viento que se mueve y gira alrededor de la tierra,
        recibe el don precioso del Espíritu.
        Amén.

23   Señor Jesucristo,
        Hijo del Dios viviente,
        ten misericordia de mí,
        pecador.

24   Te alabamos
porque nos liberaste de la muerte.
Te rogamos
que nos envíes con el pan de vida.

Te alabamos
porque hiciste que nos arrepintiéramos.
Te rogamos
que nos mantengas siempre fieles a ti.

Te alabamos
porque has comenzado tu obra de gracia.
Te rogamos
que completes en nosotros tu salvación.

Te alabamos
porque nos hiciste tu pueblo.
Te rogamos
que nos hagas uno con todos los pueblos.

25   Por medio de la fe
presentémonos ante el Dios Santo
y tomemos conciencia de lo que somos:
(oración silenciosa)

Somos el pueblo del Nuevo Cielo
y de la Nueva Tierra,
pero no vivimos de acuerdo a esa esperanza.

Somos el pueblo que recibe
la gracia de Dios,
pero no la compartimos con otros.

Pedid y recibiréis
buscad y hallaréis
llamad y se os abrirá.
Levantémonos
y vivamos
en libertad y fe.
Amén.

26   Espíritu Santo, Defensor y Consolador,
      en ti celebramos la presencia liberadora del Cristo vivo.
      Soplas donde quieres, refrescando, renovando e inspirando;
      y purificas como el fuego.

      Espíritu Santo, Defensor y Consolador,
      tú denuncias la maldad en el mundo.
      Tú revelas al mundo su pecado
      y purificas como el fuego.

      Límpianos, haznos trascender nuestros estrechos caminos.
      Defiende, preserva y cuida a tu creación,
      alimenta, sostiene y guía a tus criaturas.
      Espíritu Santo, Defensor y Consolador,
      que purificas como el fuego,
      te rogamos que nos purifiques también a nosotros.

27   Confesemos
      nuestros pecados secretos y ocultos
      que nos atemorizan y angustian
      apartándonos de Dios y de las otras personas.

      (silencio)

Korean   Jacques Berthier: Taizé France

Lord hear us. Höre uns, Gott. Ecoute nous, Dieu. Seigneur, aie pitié. Señor, escúchanos.

      Confesemos
      las denuncias que hemos rehusado expresar en nuestras sociedades,
      los acuerdos que permitieron que el mal se multiplicase
      dando como fruto la destrucción y la muerte.

      (silencio)

Korean   **Jacques Berthier: Taizé France**

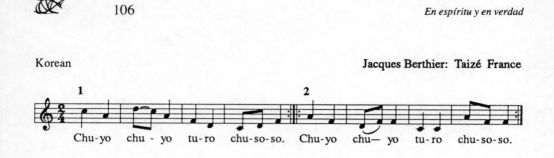

Chu-yo chu - yo tu-ro chu-so-so. Chu-yo chu— yo tu-ro chu-so-so.

Lord hear us. Höre uns, Gott. Ecoute nous, Dieu. Seigneur, aie pitié. Señor, escúchanos.

Confesemos
nuestra indiferencia en medio de la desunión,
nuestra facilidad para perpetuar prejuicios
rehusando ser el pueblo unido de Dios por el cual Jesús oró.

(silencio)

Responsorio

Dios, para quien lo íntimo del corazón es manifiesto,
todo deseo conocido y ningún secreto encubierto;
perdona nuestros pecados
y decláranos la buena nueva
de ser un pueblo liberado.

V. Colectas

28   Espíritu de verdad y de buen juicio
el único capaz de derrotar
los poderes que mantienen a nuestro mundo
al borde de la crisis, danos discernimiento
para denunciar el mal
y conocer el camino que lleva a la paz,
por Jesucristo.
Amén.

29   Oh Dios,
tú que inquietas a los satisfechos
por medio de tu verbo cargado de poder
y tus palabras veraces,
muévenos a denunciar
todo lo que distorsiona tu verdad,

y permite que nuestros corazones
estén atentos a tu voz liberadora,
en Jesucristo.
Amén.

30   Oh Dios todopoderoso, tu palabra creadora
permitió que los mares y los cielos
acogiesen toda clase de seres vivientes.
Con todos los que viven en las pequeñas islas,
nos regocijamos en la riqueza de tu creación,
y oramos para que concedas sabiduría
a todos los habitantes del planeta,
para que sepamos cuidar y no destruir
lo que tú has creado para bien de nosotros
y de nuestros descendientes.
En el nombre de Jesús oramos.
Amén.

31   Oh Dios, nuestro creador
y proveedor de todo bien,
libéranos de nuestros egoísmos
para que podamos compartir
lo que somos,
lo que sabemos,
y lo que tenemos
[en esta Asamblea] y en todo el mundo al cual amas.
Te lo pedimos en el nombre de Jesucristo
quien hace posible este compartir.
Amén.

32   Espíritu de poder y de cambio
que ungiste a Jesús
para ser la esperanza de las naciones;
desciende también sobre nosotros
sin reserva, ni distinción,
para que con confianza y fortaleza
sembremos tu justicia sobre la tierra,
por medio de Jesucristo.
Amén.

VI. Credos

33   Creemos en un solo Dios,
              Padre todopoderoso,
              Creador de cielo y tierra,
              de todo lo visible y lo invisible.

              Creemos en un solo Señor, Jesucristo,
              Hijo único de Dios,
              nacido del Padre antes de todos los siglos :
              Luz de Luz,
              Dios verdadero de Dios verdadero,
              engendrado, no creado,
              de la misma naturaleza que el Padre,
              por quien todo fue hecho ;
              que por nosotros y por nuestra salvación bajó del cielo,
              y por obra del Espíritu Santo
              se encarnó de María, la Virgen,
              y se hizo hombre ;
              y por nuestra causa fue crucificado en tiempos de Poncio Pilato ;
              padeció y fue sepultado,
              y resucitó al tercer día, según las Escrituras,
              y subió al cielo,

              y está sentado a la derecha del Padre ;
              y de nuevo vendrá con gloria
              para juzgar a vivos y muertos,
              y su reino no tendrá fin.

              Creemos en el Espíritu Santo,
              Señor y dador de vida,
              que procede del Padre ;
              que con el Padre y el Hijo
              recibe una misma adoración y gloria,
              y que habló por los profetas.
              Creemos que la Iglesia es una, santa, católica y apostólica.
              Reconocemos un solo bautismo para el perdón de los pecados.
              Esperamos la resurrección de los muertos
              y la vida del mundo futuro.
              Amén.

                       Credo Niceno - Constantinopolitano

34 Creo en Dios,
 Padre todopoderoso,
 Creador del cielo y de la tierra.

 Creo en Jesucristo,
 su único Hijo, nuestro Señor;
 que fue concebido
 por obra del Espíritu Santo,
 nació de la Virgen María;
 padeció bajo el poder de Poncio Pilato,
 fue crucificado, muerto
 y sepultado;
 descendió a los infiernos;
 al tercer día
 resucitó de entre los muertos;
 subió a los cielos
 y está sentado
 a la diestra de Dios Padre todopoderoso;
 y desde allí ha de venir a juzgar
 a los vivos y a los muertos.

 Creo en el Espíritu Santo;
 la santa iglesia católica;
 la comunión de los santos;
 el perdón de los pecados;
 la resurrección de la carne
 y la vida perdurable.
 Amén.

Credo de los apóstoles

VII. Intercesiones

35 Oh Dios, nuestro Padre,
 protege nuestras costas de las armas de la muerte,
 nuestras tierras de todo lo que priva a nuestros jóvenes del amor y la libertad.
 Permite que los mares [del Océano Pacífico]
 lleven mensajes de paz y buena voluntad.
 Quita de nuestro medio toda práctica brutal e injusta.
 Permite que nuestros hijos puedan nadar y respirar el aire fresco
 que está lleno de tu Espíritu Santo.

Oh Señor Jesús,
bendice a todos los que se esfuerzan por lograr la paz
que derriba las barreras del odio,
y únenos con los brazos abiertos de tu cruz,
para que las gentes de todo el mundo
puedan vivir por siempre juntas en armonía.
Amén.

36   Oh Dios,
dador de la vida,
te rogamos por la Iglesia en el mundo entero.
Santifica su vida, renueva su culto,
da poder a su testimonio,
restablece su unidad.
Concede tu fuerza a aquéllos que en comunión
buscan la obediencia que produce unión.
Sana las divisiones que nos separan,
para que pronto logremos la unidad del Espíritu
en el vínculo de la paz.
Amén.

37   Oh Dios
que amas la justicia y estableces la paz sobre la tierra,
hoy traemos ante ti la desunión de nuestro mundo:
la violencia absurda y las guerras que minan el ánimo de los pueblos;
el militarismo y la carrera armamentista que amenazan la vida del planeta;
la codicia humana y la injusticia que engendran el odio y el conflicto.
Envía tu Espíritu y renueva la faz de la tierra:
Enséñanos a sentir compasión y respeto hacia toda la familia humana;
fortalece a todos los que luchan por la paz y la justicia;
conduce a todas las naciones por los senderos de la paz,
y danos de esa paz que el mundo no puede dar.
Amén.

38   Señor, por la sangre derramada de tus mártires,
congrega en alegría a tus hijos esparcidos por todo el mundo,
y a todos los que lloran amargamente frente a la tristeza de la desunión,
dales la gracia de tu salvación.

39   Pidamos al Señor por la venida de su Reino.

Oh Dios, en el dolor del torturado,
infunde quietud.

El hambre del pobre,
llénala con tu plenitud.

En las heridas de nuestro planeta,
infunde bienestar.

En tus criaturas muertas,
infunde vida.

En aquéllos que te buscan con ansias,
infunde tu ser.

Venga tu reino,
hágase tu voluntad.
El Reino, el poder y la gloria
sean tuyos ahora y por siempre.

Nuestro Dios está con nosotros.

¡ Celebremos el milagro de la vida !
¡ Celebremos el milagro de la creación !
Nuestro Dios nos ama,
Nuestras vidas son una bendición de Dios,
¡ Démosle gracias con alegría !
Amén.

40   En este día, Señor, congregados como pueblo tuyo,
te pedimos que nuestro testimonio sea fiel a Jesucristo :
Danos voz para hablar por los silenciados.
Y una calma comunión
en la que sólo el silencio rinda homenaje al sufrimiento :

Danos Señor lágrimas, frente al dolor
y regocijo al experimentar el gozo de tu creación.

Danos determinación para denunciar la injusticia.
Y tu eterna bondad
hacia los desesperados que encontramos en el camino.

Danos integridad para reconocer nuestras dudas.
Que seamos fieles con nuestro prójimo
porque tú, Señor, en fidelidad y confianza nos has llamado a
servirte, sabiendo que nuestra oración es el medio de unión
de tu amor y nuestro amor por el mundo.

En la gracia de Dios yace la infinita posibilidad de esperanza.
Amén.

41   Recuerda Señor, las lluvias, las aguas y los ríos y bendícelos.

Recuerda Señor, las plantas, las semillas y los frutos que se dan en los
campos cada año, bendícelos y multiplícalos en abundancia.

Recuerda Señor, a tu santa Iglesia y a todas las ciudades y países y
protégelos.

Recuerda Señor, a la humanidad, a las bestias del campo, y a mí, tu indigna
servidora y protégenos.

Recuerda Señor, a nuestros padres y a nuestras madres, a nuestros hermanos
y hermanas que han partido y entrado en tu reposo.

Recuerda Señor, a los cautivos de tu pueblo, y haz que regresen en paz a sus
hogares.

Recuerda Señor, a los afligidos y a los que sufren.

Recuerda Señor, a tus siervos y a tus siervas, ten misericordia de los pobres
oprimidos y sostenlos en tu verdad, que tu Espíritu habite en ellos, y que el
amor y la esperanza de tu pueblo los acompañen.
Amén.

42   Oh Dios, hazte presente en medio nuestro por amor de todos los seres
humanos que habitan la tierra.
Abre nuestros ojos para que veamos tu salvación
y revélate a esta humanidad ciega.

Haz resplandecer tu rostro sobre los abatidos por la enfermedad,
dales tu fortaleza y tu paz.

Que los pobres, los débiles y todos los doblegados por la miseria
puedan conocerte para descansar y ser saciados en ti.

Concede a los poderosos y a los ricos ese poder del cual carecen.
Dales de tu discernimiento para que puedan ser libres,
libres en tu libertad, libres para amar.

A todos y a cada uno de nosotros danos de tu paz y de tu vida.
Amén.

43　　Donde la ignorancia, el egoísmo y la indiferencia
han roto la vida comunitaria,
envía tu luz, oh Dios de amor.

Donde la injusticia y la opresión han quebrantado
el espíritu de los pueblos,
envía tu luz, oh Dios liberador.

Donde el hambre y la pobreza, la enfermedad y la muerte
han vuelto la vida una carga insoportable,
envía tu luz, oh Dios de gracia.

Donde la sospecha y el odio, el conflicto y la guerra
han cuestionado tu bondad,
envía tu luz, oh Dios de paz.

Dios eterno,
abre los ojos de la naciones y los pueblos
para que puedan andar en tu luz;
extirpa de la naciones y los pueblos la ignorancia y la rebeldía,
para que puedan beber de tu fuente de bondad.
Amén.

44　　Ven, Espíritu Santo, renueva toda tu creación.
Envía el viento y el fuego
de tu poder transformador
y reaviva a tu Iglesia en este día.
Danos sabiduría y fe
para que podamos descubrir
la gran esperanza a la que nos has llamado.
Ven, Espíritu Santo,
renueva toda tu creación.

Dador de la vida,
sustenta tu creación.
Enfréntanos con
nuestro codicioso consumo de tus dones.
Hazte presente
cuando robamos y destruimos.
Suscita en nosotros
nuevas formas de cuidado
hacia todo lo que vive y respira
y existe en esta tierra.
Ven, Espíritu Santo,
renueva toda tu creación.

Espíritu de verdad,
libéranos
para actuar como hijos e hijas de Dios.
Abre nuestros oídos
para oír el gemido
del mundo.
Abre nuestros labios
para ser portavoces
de los silenciados.
Abre nuestros ojos
para compartir tu visión
de justicia y de paz.
Reanímanos con la fuerza y la fe
de tu verdad profética.
Ven, Espíritu Santo,
renueva toda tu creación.

Espíritu de unidad,
reconcilia a tu pueblo.
Danos sabiduría
para cumplir con lo necesario
para ser tu Iglesia.
Danos la gracia
para dejar
a un lado lo secundario.
Permítenos contemplar tu grandeza
para comprender nuestra pequeñez
y congréganos en humildad.
Ven, Espíritu Santo,
renueva toda tu creación.

Espíritu Santo,
transfórmanos y santifícanos
al asumir esta tarea
en tu nombre.
Concede a tu pueblo los dones necesarios
para ser tu Iglesia
en espíritu y en verdad.
Ven, Espíritu Santo,
renueva toda tu creación.

45   Señor todopoderoso,
que sanas el cuerpo y el alma,
tú que humillas y exaltas,
que castigas y perdonas,
visita en tu misericordia
a nuestros hermanos y hermanas que están enfermos.
Pon tu mano sobre ellos
y levántales del lecho del dolor.

Libérales del espíritu de enfermedad
y de todo sufrimiento, fiebre o dolencia
a los que estén sujetos;
y por tu amor a la humanidad otórgales la remisión y el perdón
de sus pecados y transgresiones
Señor, mi Dios,
ten piedad de tu creación por las misericordias de tu unigénito Hijo,
junto a tu Espíritu santísimo, todo bondad y creador de vida con quienes te
bendecimos,
ahora y siempre y por los siglos de los siglos.
Amén.

46   Acuérdate, Señor, de nuestra ciudad
            y de todas la ciudades y regiones
            y de todos los fieles que habitan en ellas.

Romania

Doam - ne mi - lu - ie - ste.   Doam - ne mi - lu - ie - ste.

Doam - ne mi - lu - ie - ste.

Kyrie eleison. Lord have mercy. Herr, erbarme dich. Seigneur, aie pitié. Señor, ten piedad.

            Acuérdate, Señor, de la seguridad de los viajeros,
            de los enfermos, de los obreros y de los que están en prisión.

            Responsorio

            Acuérdate, Señor, de aquellos que dan frutos y hacen el bien en tu
            santa iglesia y de los que recuerdan al pobre.

            Responsorio

            Derrama sobre todos nosotros las riquezas de tu misericordia,
            danos una boca y un corazón que glorifiquen y celebren
            tu glorioso y magnífico nombre, Padre, Hijo y Espíritu Santo,
            ahora y siempre y por los siglos de los siglos.

            Responsorio

            Las misericordias de Dios y de nuestro Salvador Jesucristo sean
            con todos nosotros.
            Amén.

47   Oremos al Señor.

            Porque el mundo es bello,
            y la belleza es tierna y delicada,
            y nosotros somos mayordomos de la creación,
            te necesitamos, Señor,
            te necesitamos, Señor.

            Porque el conocimiento humano parece tan vasto
            y no sabemos cuánto desconocemos,
            te necesitamos, Señor,
            te necesitamos, Señor.

Porque podemos vivir alejados de ti
y somos libres para oponernos a tus propósitos
y adorar nuestra propia sabiduría,
te necesitamos, Señor,
te necesitamos, Señor.

Porque viniste a esta tierra
y estuviste a nuestro lado,
porque experimentaste nuestro rechazo,
nos sanaste aun cuando te heríamos,
porque nos amaste hasta el fin
y triunfaste sobre el odio,
te necesitamos, Señor,
te necesitamos, Señor.
Amén.

48   Dios de la vida, te damos gracias porque nos liberaste del poder del pecado y
de la muerte. Nos enviaste a todo el mundo como señales de tu reino. Te
damos gracias por aquellos que con gracia y valentía luchan en medio de las
aflicciones del mundo para hacer visible tu luz.
Espíritu de verdad, libéranos.

Dios de la vida, por tu gracia Jesucristo iluminó nuestras vidas y todo el
mundo con su luz. Ilumina nuestros corazones para que abundemos en
esperanza. Te damos gracias por los dirigentes visionarios y creativos que
llaman a tu iglesia a vivir una nueva vida en esperanza. Inspira a todos con tu
Espíritu para que sean liberados a una nueva vida en esperanza.
Espíritu de verdad, libéranos.

Dios de la vida, te damos gracias por los hombres y mujeres de fe que a
través de la historia respondieron a tu llamado a la libertad y a la vida. Abre
nuestros ojos y despierta nuestros oídos para verte y oírte obrando en el
mundo y en nuestras vidas. Derriba las barreras que esclavizan y dividen a la
gente y libéralos para vivir una vida abundante.
Espíritu de verdad, libéranos.

49   Espíritu de paz, llena toda la creación con tu presencia transformadora. Que
todos los gobernantes sean maduros y justos en sus gestiones. Que todas la
naciones gocen de tranquilidad y que sus hijos e hijas sean benditos. Que los
pueblos, los rebaños y ganados prosperen y se vean libres de toda enfermedad. Que los campos produzcan fruto en abundancia y que la tierra sea fértil.
Que todos los enemigos busquen la paz.

From "Missa da Terra Sem Males"   D. Pedro Casaldáliga, Pedro Tierra, Martín Coplas:
                                                        Guarany, Brazil--Paraguay

Sha - lom,   sa - wi-di,   a paz.   Sha-lom,   sa- wi- di,   a paz.

Peace Friede Paix Paz

Espíritu de Unidad, oramos por tu iglesia. Cólmala de toda paz y verdad.
Donde haya corrupción, purifícala; donde haya error, guíala; donde falle,
refórmala; donde esté acertada, fortalécela; donde esté en necesidad,
sáciala; donde esté dividida, únela.

Responsorio

Espíritu de amor, vela por los que están en vigilia o de guardia o los que
lloran, y envía a tus ángeles que guarden el sueño de los que duermen. Cuida
a los enfermos, da descanso a los fatigados, da valor a las mujeres en trabajo
de parto, mitiga el sufrimiento, y bendice a los que están muriendo....

Responsorio

50   En un mundo dominado por imágenes de guerra,
       libéranos de la esclavitud del conflicto.

       En un mundo que levanta barreras divisorias,
       libéranos de la esclavitud del racismo.

       Haz que nosotros que no éramos pueblo
       nos transformemos en una comunidad viviente siendo tu pueblo.
       Danos un solo corazón y un alma
       para compartir todo lo que tenemos.

VIII. Bendiciones

51   Oremos:
       Señor Jesucristo,
       porque compartiste el pan con el pobre
       te despreciaron.

       Porque compartiste el pan con los pecadores
       y los despreciados te consideraron impío.

Porque compartiste el pan con alegría
te llamaron glotón y bebedor.

Porque al compartir el pan en el aposento alto
confirmaste tu decisión de seguir el camino de la cruz.

Porque al compartir el pan en el camino a Emaús
abriste los ojos de tus discípulos.
Porque tú partiste el pan y lo compartiste,
nosotros también lo hacemos
y pedimos tu bendición.

Señor Jesús,
bendice este pan
y a las personas con quienes lo compartimos.
Renueva nuestra vida comunitaria,
para que podamos compartir tu Palabra el uno con el otro,
y en el diario trajinar sintamos arder nuestros corazones.
Amén.

52   Vayan con la fortaleza que tienen
Vayan humildemente,
    sin cargas,
    mansamente,
en busca de amor.
Que el Espíritu de Dios vaya con Uds.

53   Dios de poder,
que la osadía de tu Espíritu nos transforme,
que la dulzura de tu Espíritu nos dirija,
que los dones de tu Espíritu nos capaciten
para servirte y adorarte
ahora y siempre.
Por medio de Jesucristo nuestro Señor.
Amén.

54   Amado Señor, ayúdanos a no ser violentos en nuestro afán de conservación,
a obrar sin buscar el reconocimiento
a llegar a la meta sin afanarnos por ello,
para que todo lo que hagamos
te glorifique.
Amén.

55   Que Dios Todopoderoso te bendiga;
      que las bendiciones del cielo
      y las de las profundidades de la tierra,
      las bendiciones de los pechos y de los vientres,
      las bendiciones de los granos y de las flores,
      las bendiciones de las eternas montañas,
      riqueza de las colinas sempiternas
      sean contigo y te acompañen;
      en el nombre del Padre, del Hijo y del Espíritu Santo.
      Amén.

56   Vayan en paz.
      Que el Santo Dios los sorprenda
      en el camino,
      que Jesucristo los acompañe
      y el Espíritu alce vuestros pies.
      Amén.

57   Que el Dios de Amor que compartió su amor
            nos fortalezca para amar a otros.
      Que el Hijo que compartió su vida
            nos dé la gracia de compartir la nuestra.
      Que el Espíritu Santo que habita en nosotros
            nos fortalezca para que
            siempre nos entreguemos a los demás.
      Amén.

58   Dios Eternal,
      nuestro principio y fin,
      sé nuestro punto de partida y nuestro paraíso eterno
      y acompáñanos al recorrer este día.
      Usa nuestras manos
      para llevar a cabo la obra de tu creación
      y usa nuestras vidas
      para llevar a otros la nueva vida que das al mundo
      en Jesucristo, Redentor del universo.
      Amén.

**Hymns and
liturgical responses**

**Lieder und
liturgische Responsorien**

**Cantiques et
répons liturgiques**

**Himnos y
responsorios litúrgicos**

Index of first lines
Verzeichnis der Liedanfänge
Répertoire des titres
Lista de títulos

*Page/Seite/page/página

Caroline Rockson: Ghana **1**

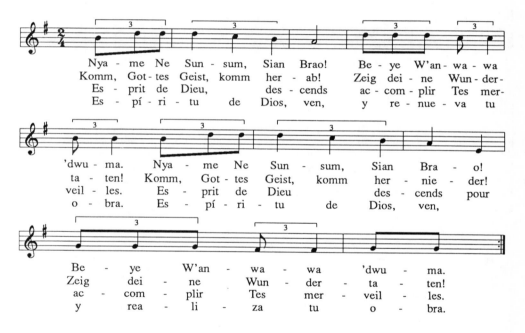

Nya - me Ne Sun - sum, Sian Brao! Be - ye W'an - wa - wa
Komm, Got - tes Geist, komm her - ab! Zeig dei - ne Wun - der -
Es - prit de Dieu, des - cends ac - com - plir Tes mer -
Es - pí - ri - tu de Dios, ven, y re - nue - va tu

'dwu - ma. Nya - me Ne Sun - sum, Sian Bra - o!
ta - ten! Komm, Got - tes Geist, komm her - nie - der!
veil - les. Es - prit de Dieu des - cends pour
o - bra. Es - pí - ri - tu de Dios, ven,

Be - ye W'an - wa - wa 'dwu - ma.
Zeig dei - ne Wun - der - ta - ten!
ac - com - plir Tes mer - veil - les.
y rea - li - za tu o - bra.

Spirit of God come down and perform your wonderful works.

Jacques Berthier: Taizé, France **2**

Ve - ni Cre - a - tor, Ve - ni Cre - a - tor, Ve - ni Cre - a - tor Spi - ri - tus.

Come Creator Spirit. Komm Schöpfer Geist. Viens Esprit Créateur. Ven Espíritu Creador.

3 Prayer to the Holy Spirit   Russia

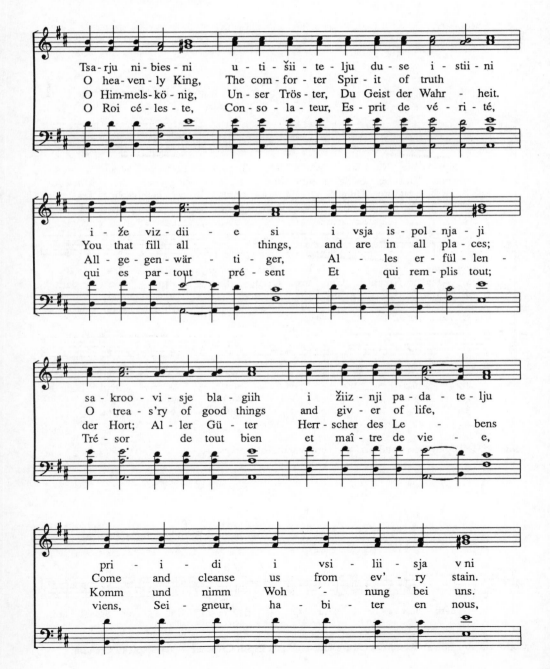

Tsa - rju ni - bies - ni   u - ti - šii - te - lju du - se i - stii - ni
O hea - ven - ly King,   The com - for - ter Spir - it of truth
O Him - mels - kö - nig, Un - ser Trös - ter, Du Geist der Wahr - heit.
O Roi cé - les - te,   Con - so - la - teur, Es - prit de vé - ri - té,

i - že viz - dii - e si   i vsja is - pol - nja - ji
You that fill all   things,   and are in all pla - ces;
All - ge - gen - wär - ti - ger,   Al - les er - fül - len -
qui es par - tout pré - sent Et qui rem - plis tout;

sa - kroo - vi - sje bla - giih   i žiiz - nji pa - da - te - lju
O trea - s'ry of good things   and giv - er of life,
der Hort; Al - ler Gü - ter   Herr - scher des Le - bens
Tré - sor de tout bien   et maî - tre de vie - e,

pri - i - di i   vsi - lii - sja v ni
Come and cleanse us from ev' - ry stain.
Komm und nimm Woh - nung bei uns.
viens, Sei - gneur, ha - bi - ter en nous,

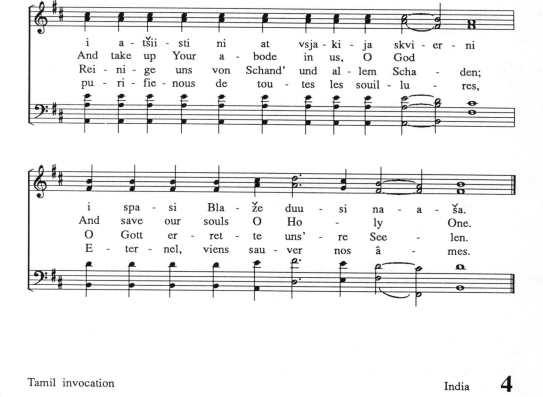

i a - tšii - sti ni at vsja - ki - ja skvi - er - ni
And take up Your a - bode in us, O God
Rei - ni - ge uns von Schand' und al - lem Scha - den;
pu - ri - fie - nous de tou - tes les souil - lu - res,

i spa - si Bla - že duu - si na - a - ša.
And save our souls O Ho - ly One.
O Gott er - ret - te uns' - re See - len.
E - ter - nel, viens sau - ver nos â - mes.

Tamil invocation India 4

Va - ra - vë - num pa - ran ä - vi - yë I - ran - kum su-da - räi më - vi - yë.
Ho - ly Spi - rit, de-scend up-on us. Come down, as a flam - ing fire.

Heiliger Geist, komm zu uns hernieder, komm über uns wie ein flammendes Feuer.
Saint-Esprit viens sur nous comme un feu brûlant.
Espíritu Santo desciende sobre nosotros. Ven, desciende como una llama de fuego.

5

Wilson Niwagila: Tanzania

Njo-o kwe-tu, Ro-ho Mwe-ma, M-fa-ri-ji-wa-tu. Tu-fu-
Come a-mong us, lov-ing Spir-it, touch us and make us whole. Show us
Komm zu uns, Hei-li-ger Geist, Du der Du Trös-ter heisst: Lehr' uns

ndi-she ya mbi-ngu-ni. Tu-we wa-tu wa-pya.
glimp-ses of the King-dom, use us to spread its rule.
die Macht des Him-mels Sie macht uns Men-schen neu.

Refrain

Njo-o, njo-o, njoo, Ro-ho Mwe-ma.
Lov-ing Spir-it, fill us with your life.
Komm, komm, zu uns Heil'-ger Geist.

2. Utufanye waamini/ Wa Yesu Mwokozi./ Tukaishi kikundini,/ Kanisani mwako.

3. Kwa huruma tubariki,/ Tuishi na wewe./ Tukatende kila kitu/ Kuongozwa nawe.

4. Roho Mwema, Mfariji,/ Utupe hekima;/ Tukiwaza na kutenda,/ Yote yawe yako.

5. Tudumishe,tuwe hai/ Na ukweli wako./ Tusivutwe na dunia,/ Tushu'die neema.

2. Loving Spirit, come and kindle/ faith in our Lord, God's Son./ Make your people in their worship/ and in their action one.

3. Spirit, bless us with awareness/ that you are down-to-earth./ Give us courage, bring among us/ love like a child to birth.

4. Loving Spirit, let your wisdom/ guide what we think and do./ Make us willing and responsive/ as you make all things new.

5. From the grip of fear and conflict,/ Spirit! your world release./ Help your people to discover/ things that will make for peace.

2. Mach uns frei in frohem Glauben/ der Christi Heil erfasst/ in Gemeinschaft so zu leben/ wie Du geboten hast.

3. Bleibe bei uns, führe Du uns,/ gnädig in allem Tun:/ Dein Erbarmen uns bestimme/ täglich in unserm Mühn.

4. Geist der Güte, wahrer Tröster,/ Du bist der Weisheit Quell./ Unser Herz füll, unsre Sinnen,/ mach unsre Augen hell.

5. Deine Fülle gibt uns Leben,/ Wahrheit und Weg und Ziel,/ Mut und Freude willst Du geben:/ Boten Christi sind wir.

as taught be Samuel Solanke: Yoruba, Nigeria   **6**

Wa   Wa   Wa   E - mi - mi - mo,
Come,   O   Ho - ly Spir - it   come.
Komm,   o   komm Hei - li - ger Geist.
O   viens,   Es -   prit,   viens,

Tenor solo

E - mi - o - lo - ye
O wise Spir - it come.
du Geist der Wahr - heit
Es - prit de   sa - gesse

Wa   Wa   Wa   A - lag - ba - ra
Come,   al - might - y Spir - it Come,
Komm,   o   komm du Geist voll Kraft.
O   viens,   puis - sant Es - prit, viens,

a - lag - ba - ra - me - ta
al - might - y Tri - ni - ty
du   Geist der Ei - nig - keit
Puis - san - te Tri - ni - té

Wa - o   wa - o   wa - o.
Come,   come,   come.
Komm,   Komm,   Komm.
Viens,   viens,   viens.

E - mi - mi - mo.
O   Spir - it, come.
Hei - li - ger Geist.
O   Es - prit, viens.

7   Kiowa prayer, paraphrased by Libby Littlechief   Kiowa melody: USA

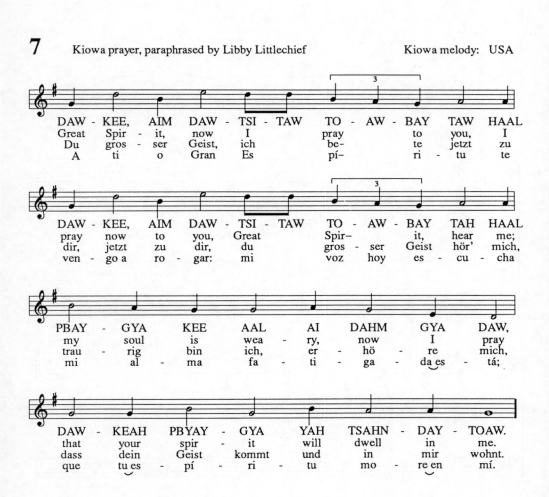

DAW - KEE, AIM DAW - TSI - TAW TO - AW - BAY TAW HAAL
Great Spir - it, now I pray to you, I
Du gros - ser Geist, ich be- te jetzt zu
A ti o Gran Es pí- ri - tu te

DAW - KEE, AIM DAW - TSI - TAW TO - AW - BAY TAH HAAL
pray now to you, Great Spir- it, hear me;
dir, jetzt zu dir, du gros - ser Geist hör' mich;
ven - go a ro - gar: mi voz hoy es - cu - cha

PBAY - GYA KEE AAL AI DAHM GYA DAW,
my soul is wea - ry, now I pray
trau - rig bin ich, er - hö - re mich,
mi al - ma fa - ti - ga - da es - tá;

DAW - KEAH PBYAY - GYA YAH TSAHN - DAY - TOAW.
that your spir - it will dwell - in me.
dass dein Geist kommt und in mir wohnt.
que tu es - pí - ri - tu mo - re en mí.

Alexander Gondo: Shona, Zimbabwe **8**

U - ya - i - mo - se ti - na - ma - te Mwa - ri,
Come all you peo - ple, Come and wor - ship Yah - weh,
Kommt, all ihr Men - schen, ruft ihn an un - sern Gott,
O vous, bon - nes gens, ve - nez a - do - rer Dieu,

U - ya - i - mo - se ti - na - ma - te Mwa - ri,
Come all you peo - ple, Come and wor - ship Yah - weh
Kommt, all ihr Men - schen, ruft ihn an un - sern Gott,
O vous, bon - nes gens, ve - nez a - do - rer Dieu,

U - ya - i - mo - se ti - na - ma - te Mwa - ri,
Come all you peo - ple, Come and wor - ship Yah - weh
Kommt, all ihr Men - schen, ruft ihn an un - sern Gott,
O vous, bon - nes gens, ve - nez a - do - rer Dieu,

U - ya - i mo - se zvi - no.
Come now and wor - ship the Lord.
Kommt jetzt und be - tet ihn an!
ve - nez a - do - rer Dieu.

Psalm 100:1,2 Gottfried Rüger: Germany **9**

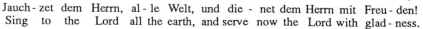

Jauch - zet dem Herrn, al - le Welt, und die - net dem Herrn mit Freu - den!
Sing to the Lord all the earth, and serve now the Lord with glad - ness.

10 Psalm 68:26 Pidgin   Traditional: Papua New Guinea

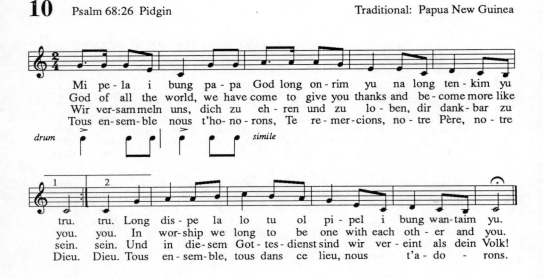

Mi pe-la i bung pa-pa God long on-rim yu na long ten-kim yu
God of all the world, we have come to give you thanks and be-come more like
Wir ver-sam-meln uns, dich zu eh-ren und zu lo-ben, dir dank-bar zu
Tous en-sem-ble nous t'ho-no-rons, Te re-mer-cions, no-tre Père, no-tre

drum ... *simile*

tru. tru. Long dis-pe la lo tu ol pi-pel i bung wan-taim yu.
you. you. In wor-ship we long to be one with each oth-er and you.
sein. sein. Und in die-sem Got-tes-dienst sind wir ver-eint als dein Volk!
Dieu. Dieu. Tous en-sem-ble, tous dans ce lieu, nous t'a-do-rons.

11 Luke 2:14   Pablo Sosa: Argentina

Cueca

Glo-ria, glo-ria, glo-ria en las al-tu-ras a Dios.
Eh-re, Eh-re, Eh-re, Eh-re im Him-mel sei Gott.
Gloi-re, Gloi-re, Gloi-re, à Dieu dans les lieux très-hauts.

Y en la tie-rra paz pa-ra a-que-llos que a-ma el Se-ñor.
Und auf Er-den Friede un-ter de-nen, die ihn lie-ben.
Sur la ter-re paix à ceux qui ai-ment le Sei-gneur.

Peru **12**

Glo - ria a Dios, Glo - ria a Dios, Glo - ria en los cie - los!
Glo - ry to God, Glo - ry to God, Glo - ry in the high - est!
Eh - re sei Gott, Eh - re sei Gott, Eh - re in der Hö - he!
Gloire à Dieu, Gloire à Dieu, à Dieu Gloi - re dans les hauts - lieux!

A Dios la glo - ria por siem - pre! Al - le - lu - ya, A - men!
To God be glo - ry for - e - ver!
Gott sei Eh - re für im - mer!
Gloire au Sei - gneur, gloire à ja - mais!

Al - le - lu - ya, A - men! Al - le - lu - ya, A - men!

2. Gloria a Dios, Gloria a Dios, Gloria a Jesucristo. . .

3. Gloria a Dios, Gloria a Dios, Gloria sea al Espíritu. . .

2. Glory to God, Glory to God, Glory to Christ Jesus. . .

3. Glory to God, Glory to God, Glory to the Spirit. . .

2. Ehre sei Gott, Ehre sei Gott, Ehre sei Dir, Jesus. . .

3. Ehre sei Gott, Ehre sei Gott, Ehre sei dem Geiste. . .

2. Gloire à Dieu, Gloire à Dieu, Gloire au Seigneur Jésus. . .

3. Gloire à Dieu, Gloire à Dieu, Gloire à l'Esprit très saint. . .

13 Doxology   Greece

Andante

Tho - xa   Si   to   thi - xan - ti   to   fos.
Glo - ry   to   God,   who   gives   us   light.
Gloi - re,   Gloire   à   Dieu   pour   la   lu - mière,

Tho - xa   en   ip - sis - tis   The - o.   Ka   e - pi   gis   i - ri—   ni
Glo - ry   in   the   high - est   to   God.   And   on   the   earth   may   peace   reign
Gloire   à   Dieu   dans   les   hauts   lieux.   Et   sur   la   ter - re,   paix   au

en   an - thro - pis   ev - tho - ki—   a.   A - gi - os   o   The - os.   A - gi - os   Is - ki - ros.
a - mong   peo - ple   of   good—   will.
peu - ple   de   bon - ne   vo - lon—   té.

A - gi - os   A - tha - na - tos   e - le - i - son   i - mas.

Basses articulate text on note C (Do), sustained throughout.

Refrain:
Holy God, Holy Mighty, Holy Immortal: Have mercy on us.

Dieu saint, saint et fort, saint et immortel, aie pitié de nous.

Heiliger Gott, heiliger Mächtiger, heiliger Unsterblicher, erbarme dich unser.

Santo Dios, Santo Poderoso, Santo Immortal, ¡Ten misericordia de nosotros!

Jacques Berthier: Taizé France **14**

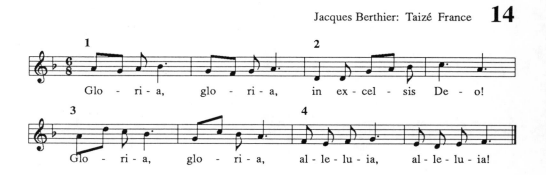

Glory to God in the highest. Ehre sei Gott in der Höhe. Gloire à Dieu au plus haut des cieux.
Gloria a Dios en el cielo

Mt. Athos Melody: Greece **15**

Lord, have mercy. Herr, erbarme dich. Seigneur, aie pitié de nous. Señor, ten piedad de nosotros.

Dinah Reindorf: Ghana **16**

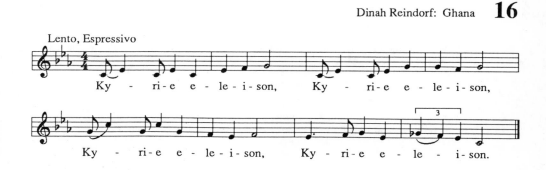

17

Jaci C. Maraschin: Brazil

nhor,   tem   pie - da - de de nós.
ñor,   ten   pie - dad de no - so–tros.
Lord,   have   mer - cy on us.
gneur, aie pi - tié de nous.

G. M. Kolisi: South Africa **18**

Nko - si, Nko - si, yi - ba nen - ce - ba.
Lord have mer - cy, have mer - cy up - on us.
Dieu aie pi - tié, aie pi - tié de nous.
Ten   pie - dad Se - ñor de no - so - tros.

Kres - tu, Kres - tu, yi - ba nen - ce - ba.
Christ have mer - cy, have mer - cy up - on us.
Christ aie pi - tié, aie pi - tié de nous.
Ten   pie - dad Cris - to de no - so - tros.

19

Armenia

Der, vo - ghor - mia, Der, vo - ghor - mia,
Ky - rie e - lei - son, Ky - rie e - lei - son,

Der,
Ky

Der vo - ghor - mia,
Ky - rie e - lei - son,

Der, vo - ghor - mia, Der, vo - ghor - mia.
Ky - rie e - lei - son, Ky - rie e - lei - son.

Der vo - ghor - mia.
Ky - rie e - lei - son,

rie

Der vo - ghor - mia,
Ky - rie e - lei-son,

Der vo - ghor - mia, Der vo - ghor - mia,
Ky - rie e - lei - son, Ky - rie e - lei - son,

Caribbean **20**

Hal-le-Hal-le-Hal - le - lu - ja. Hal-le-Hal-le-Hal - le - lu - ja.

Hal-le-Hal-le-Hal - le - lu - ja. Hal-le - lu-ja, Hal - le - lu - ja.

Dinah Reindorf: Ghana **21**

Hal-le - lu - jah! Hal-le - lu - jah! Hal-le-lu-jah!

Hal-le - lu - jah! Hal-le - lu - jah! Hal - le-lu - jah!

22   Russia

Al - le - lu - ja, Al - le - lu - ja, Al - le - lu - ja!

23   Simei Monteiro: Brazil

A - le - lu - ia, A - le - lu - ia, A - le - lu - ia, ia.

24   Christian I. Tamaela: Indonesia

Pu - ji Tu - han, Pu - ji Tu - han, Pu - ji Tu - han.
Hal - le - lu - ia, Hal le - lu - ia, Hal - le - lu - ia.

South Africa **25**
arr. Betty Pulkingham

San-na,* san-na-ni-na, san-na, san-na, san-.na, san-

na, san-na, san-na, san-na-ni-na, san-na, san-na, san-na. San— na.

*Hosanna

Argentina **26**

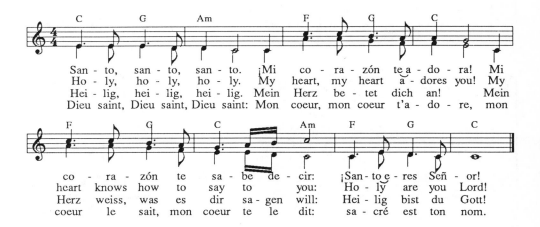

San - to, san - to, san - to. ¡Mi co - ra - zón te a - do - ra! Mi
Ho - ly, ho - ly, ho - ly. My heart, my heart a - dores you! My
Hei - lig, hei - lig, hei - lig. Mein Herz be - tet dich an! Mein
Dieu saint, Dieu saint, Dieu saint: Mon coeur, mon coeur t'a - do - re, mon

co - ra - zón te sa - be de - cir: ¡San - to e - res Señ - or!
heart knows how to say to you: Ho - ly are you Lord!
Herz weiss, was es dir sa - gen will: Hei - lig bist du Gott!
coeur le sait, mon coeur te le dit: sa - cré est ton nom.

27   The Iona Community: United Kingdom

Ho - ly   Ho - ly   Ho - ly Lord of   power and might.
Hei - lig,   Hei - lig,   Hei - lig ist Gott Herr   Ze - ba - oth.
Dieu saint,   Dieu saint,   Dieu saint Sei - gneur   tout - puis - sant,
San - to,   san - to,   san - to y po - de - ro - so Dios.

Ho - ly   Ho - ly Ho - ly Lord of   power and might.

Hea - ven   earth,   hea - ven and earth are
Him - mel,   Er - de,   Him - mel und Erd' sind
les cieux,   la terr',   les cieux, la terr' sont rem
Cie - lo,   tie - rra,   to - do es - tá lle - no

Heav - en   earth,   hea - ven and earth are

full   of   your   glo - ry.   All glo-ry to your name.
voll   sei - ner   Eh - re.   Lob-sin-get sei-nem Na - men.
plis   de   ta   gloi - re.   Gloi-re, gloi-re à ton nom.
de   tu   glo - ria.   A tu nom-bre glo - ria,

full   of   your   glo - ry.   All   glo - ry to your

All   glo - ry to your name,   Bless - ed,
Lob - sin - get sei - nem Na - men.   Preist ihn,
Gloi - re, gloi - re à ton nom.   Bé - ni,
A   tu nom - bre glo - ria,   Fe - liz,

name.   All   glo - ry to your name,   Bless - ed

28

Misa Popular Salvadoreña: El Salvador

Muy movido

F

Santo, Santo, Santo, Santo, Santo, San - to es nues - tro
Ho - ly, Ho - ly, Ho - ly, Ho - ly, Ho - ly, Ho - ly is our
Hei - lig, Hei - lig, Hei - lig, Hei - lig, Hei - lig, Hei - lig, un - ser
Très saint, Très saint, Très saint, Très saint, Très saint, Très saint, no - tre

C7

Dios, Se - ñor de to - da la tie - rra, San - to, San - to es nues - tro
God, God the Lord of earth and hea - ven, Ho - ly Ho - ly is our
Gott, Gott des Him - mels und der Er - de. Hei - lig, Hei - lig, un - ser
Dieu Sei - gneur de tou - te la ter - re, Très saint, Très saint, no - tre

F   F

Dios, San - to, San - to, San - to, San - to, San - to, San - to es nues - tro
God. Ho - ly, Ho - ly, Ho - ly, Ho - ly, Ho - ly, Ho - ly is our
Gott. Hei - lig, Hei - lig, Hei - lig, Hei - lig, Hei - lig, Hei - lig, un - ser
Dieu. Très saint, Très saint, Très saint, Très saint, Très saint, Très saint, no - tre

Fine

C7   F

Dios, Se - ñor de to - da la his - to - ria San - to San - to es nues - tro Dios.
God, God the Lord of all of his - tory, Ho - ly, Ho - ly is our God.
Gott, Gott, der Herr uns 'rer Ge - schich - te, Hei - lig, Hei - lig, un - ser Gott.
Dieu Sei - gneur de tou - te l'his - toi - re, Très saint, Très saint, no - tre Dieu

Introducción y Final

29

Per Harling: Sweden

Samba **Part 1**

Dm　　　Gm　　C7　　FM7

Du är he - lig, Du är hel. Du är all - tid myck - et mer, än vi
You are ho - ly, you are whole. You are al - ways ev - er more than we
Du bist hei - lig, hei - lig Herr, und du bist un - sag - bar mehr, mehr als
Tu es saint et a - bon - dance, et tu es tou - te - puis - sance, plus que
E - res san - to, e - res Dios por to - da la e - ter - ni - dad; siem - pre

Bb　　　Gm　　Asus4　　A7

nån - sin kan för - stå, Du är nä - ra än - då. Väl—
ev - er un - der - stand. You are al - ways at hand. Bless - ed
je ein Au - ge sah, und doch kommst du uns nah. Lob sei
nous ne com - pre - nons, En toi nous nous con - fions, Bé - nis
tu muy cer - ca es - tas de tu pueblo, buen Se - ñor. Te a - la -

Dm　　　Gm　　C7　　FM7

sig - nad va - re Du, Som kom - mer hit just nu, Väl—
are you com - ing near. Bless - ed are you com - ing here to your
dir, Du kommst zur Welt, kommst in Dei - nes Vol - kes Zelt, kommst zu
ton pro - chain re - tour, en nos â - mes ton la - bour, Pour ton
ba - mos hoy a - quí, te a - do - ra - mos con fer - vor. A tu i -

Bb　　　Gm　　A7　　Dm **Part 2**

sig - nan - de vår jord, Blir till bröd på vår jord. Du är
church in wine and bread, raised from soil, raised from dead. You are
uns in Wein und Brot, bringst uns Le - ben statt Tod. Du bist
peuple le pain, le vin de la terr' ca - deau di - vin. Tu es
gle - sia en vi - no y pan nue - va vi - da a - sí le das. E - res

Gm　　C7　　FM7　　Bb　　Gm

he - lig, Du är hel - het, Du är när - het, He - la
ho - ly, You are whole - ness, you are pre - sent, Let the
hei - lig, ganz und gar, Du bist nah, al - le
saint, plé - ni - tu - de, tu es pré - sent, que l'u -
san - to, e - res Dios, Te sen - ti - mos. La cre -

kos - mos lo - var Dig! Hal-le - lu-ja, hal-le - lu-ja, hal-le-
cos - mos praise you, Lord! Hal-le - lu-ja, hal-le - lu-ja, hal-le-
Welt, sie singt dir Lob: Hal-le - lu-ja, hal-le - lu-ja, hal-le-
ni - vers te loue Sei - gneur. Al-le - lu-ia, al-le - lu-ia, al-le-
a - ción te dé loor A - le - lu-ya, a - le - lu-ya, a - le-

lu - ja, hal - le - lu - ha, vår Gud.
lu - ja, hal - le - lu - ja, our Lord.
lu - ja, hal - le - lu - ja lobt Gott.
lu - ia, al - le - lu - ia, Sei - gneur.
lu - ya, a - le - lu - ya, Se - ñor.

Parts 1 and 2 can be sung at the same time. Teile 1 und 2 können gleichzeitig gesungen werden. Les deux parties peuvent se chanter en même temps. Las partes 1 y 2 se pueden cantar al mismo tiempo.

I-to Loh: Taiwan **30**

Giv - er of life, sus - tain Your cre - a - tion.
Du Le - bens - grund, be - schüt–ze dei - ne Schöp - fung.
O Dieu de vie, sou - tiens Ta cré - a - tion.
Oh Cre - a - dor, sos - tén tu cre - a - ción.

31 Olov Hartman   Bertil Hallin: Sweden

Leader

Gud ska-pa-de de kla-ra vatt-nen och tän-de liv med de-ras
God made the crys-tal clear wa-ters and there was land for rain to
L'eau viv', et la pluie sur les champs qui tom-be au prin-temps. Dieu les
Dios hi-zo al a-gua cris-ta-li-na, la tie-rra don-de cae la

sy-re, och vin-dar blås-te ö-ver ha-vet. Gud såg att det var gott.
fall on. The Spir-it moved up-on the o-cean. God saw that it was good.
cré-a, Son Es-prit se mou-vait sur l'on-de, Dieu vit que c'é-tait bon.
llu-via. Su Es-pí-ri-tu so-bre los ma-res. Dios vio que e-ra bueno.

Refrain All

Gud såg att det var gott. Och det vart af-ton och det vart mor-gon.
God saw that it was good, And there was eve-ning and there was morn-ing.
Dieu vit que c'é-tait bon. Et il y eut un soir et un ma-tin.
Dios vio que e-ra bueno, y fue la no-che y la ma-ña-na.

2. Gud vävde gräsets gröna matta/ med starr och hundkäx och violer/ i väldiga och skira mönster./ Gud såg att det var gott.

3. Och havet vimlade av fiskar/ och luften vimlade av fåglar/ och se, vad fjärilar på ängen!/ Gud såg att det var gott.

4. Ett ord, ett öga--allting föddes/ i människan till namn och tanke/ och talade med Gud på jorden./ Gud såg att det var gott.

5. Men fåglar dör och gräset vissnar/ och vattnet grumlas i var källa/ där människan går fram på jorden./ Gud såg att det var ont./   **Alla** Gud såg att det var ont./ Och det vart afton och det vart morgon.

6. Det gamla skapelseförbundet/ med jord och himmel ligger brutet/ --en ovän kom och gjorde detta./ Gud såg att det var ont.

7. När Jesus gick omkring ibland oss/ och gjorde väl och hjälpte alla/ förstod vi hur det var från början./ Gud såg att det var gott./   **Alla** Gud såg att det var gott./ Och det vart afton och det vart morgon.

8. En reningseld är tänd i världen,/ ett nytt förbund med jord och himmel/ är stiftat i ett bröd som brytes./ Gud såg att det var gott.

9. Gud skapar allt på nytt i Kristus/ som älskar syndaren och sparven/ och ger en öppen rymd åt båda./ Gud såg att det var gott.

2. God wove the tapestry of green grass,/ embroided flowers, bees and mushrooms,/ and fashioned trees within the garden./ God saw that it was good.

3. God made the fish and life of oceans/ and all the birds that fly above us./ On land there were all kinds of creatures./ God saw that it was good.

4. A man, a woman in God's image,/ in full communion with creation,/ were loving, sharing with each other./ God saw that it was good.

5. But birds are dying, grass is withering/ and poisoned waters kill our children./ The paradise is lost for profit./ God saw the goodness lost./   **All** God saw the goodness lost/ and there was evening and there was morning.

6. The covenant of all creation/ between the earth and heav'n is broken./ The earth is ruled by hate and evil./ God saw the goodness lost.

7. When Jesus walked his way among us/ we were reminded of God's image/ and how it was from the beginning./ God saw that it was good./   **All** God saw that it was good./ and there was evening and there was morning.

8. The Spirit's fire burns within us/ to care again for all creation/ in covenant of bread that's broken./ God saw that it was good.

9. All things will be renewed in Jesus,/ who loves both sinners and creation./ Our future will be life forever./ God saw that it was good.

2. Tissage vert, herbe des prés,/ tulip' et scarabées. Dieu les créa./ Dans le jardin, mit le grand chêne,/
Dieu vit que c'était bon.

3. Des poissons tout plein les étangs,/ merles et papillons, Dieu les créa./ Des bêtes partout sur la terre,/ Dieu vit que c'était bon.

4. A son image Dieu les fit,/ homme, femme, pleine communion,/ aimant et partageant ensemble,/ Dieu vit que c'était bon.

5. Les oiseaux meurent, l'herbe est brûlée,/ l'eau souillée détruit tous nos enfants/ paradis perdu à nos profits./ Dieu ne voit plus le bien./   **Refrain** Dieu ne voit plus le bien./ Et il y eut un soir et un matin.

6. Alliance brisée de l'univers/ où la terra bafoue son Créateur:/ la haine, le mal sont ses maîtres./ Dieu ne voit plus le bien.

7. Quand Jésus parmi nous descendit/ image réelle du Dieu vivant,/ commencement de nos mémoires./ Dieu vit que c'était bon./   **Refrain** Dieu vit que c'était bon./ Et il y eut un soir et un matin.

8. Le feu de l'Esprit nous invite/ à prendre soin de la création,/ à rompre le pain de l'alliance./ Dieu vit que c'était bon.

9. Voici toute chose est nouvelle/ pour le pécheur, pour la création./ En Christ est la vie éternelle./ Dieu vit que c'était bon.

2. Tejió después verdes alfombras,/ bordó las flores y los frutos, los árboles plantó en su huerto./ Dios vio que era bueno.

3. Les dio los peces a los mares/ y al cielo regaló las aves./ Llenó la tierra de animales./ Dios vio que era bueno.

4. La humanidad creó a su imagen,/ mujer y hombre en comunión/ su amor comparten, sus cuidados./ Dios vio que era bueno.

5. La creación, los niños mueren,/ contaminados son los mares,/ el paraíso se ha estropeado./ Lo bueno se acabó./ **Refrán** Lo bueno se acabó./ y fue la noche y la mañana.

6. El pacto hecho entre lo eterno/ y lo terreno ahora es roto./ El mal gobierna en todas partes./ Lo bueno se acabó. **Refrán** Lo bueno se acabó. . .

7. Cuando Jesús entró en la historia,/ nos recordó de nuestro orígen:/ creados por Dios, a su imágen./ Dios vio que era bueno.

8. Cuando el Espíritu nos toca/ volvemos a cuidar la tierra/ en conpromiso y esperanza./ Dios vio que era bueno.

9. En Jesucristo se renueva/ la creación, la humanidad, la vida./ Ya disfrutamos de futuro./ Dios vio que era bueno.

Ramon & Sario Oliano: Kalahan
Psalm 24:1

Ikalahan melody: Philippines **32**

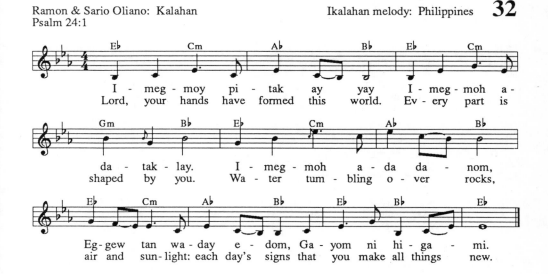

I - meg - moy pi - tak ay yay I - meg - moh a -
Lord, your hands have formed this world. Ev - ery part is

da - tak - lay. I - meg - moh a - da da - nom,
shaped by you. Wa - ter tum - bling o - ver rocks,

Eg- gew tan wa - day e - dom, Ga - yom ni hi - ga - mi.
air and sun- light: each day's signs that you make all things new.

2. Pantaneman ipitak/ Taklay i mangitodak,/ Danom i an manibog./ Eggew i on dada od Gayom ni hi-gami.

3. Ambel-at i kayabang/ Tep obimi aateng./ Dakel iday manokmi,/ Tan matabay killomi,/ Gayom ni hi-gami.

2. Yours the soil that holds the seed,/ you give warmth and moisture, too./ Sprouting crops and blossom buds, trees and plants: the seasons' signs/ that you make all things new.

3. We search out new ground to weed,/ even mountain fields will do./ You uproot the toughest sins/ from our souls: both steward signs/ that you make all things new.

33 Nobuaki Hanaoka

Traditional melody 'Sakura': Japan

Praise the Lord, praise the Lord, for the green - ness
Lobt unsern Gott, lobt unsern Gott. Für das Grün von
Lou - ez Dieu, lou - ez Dieu pour la sè - ve
A - la - bad al Se - ñor por los ár - bo -

of the trees, for the beau - ty of the flow'rs,
Blatt und Baum, für der Blu - men schö - ne Pracht,
dans l'ar - bre, pour le par - fum de la fleur,
les en flor, de mag - ní - fi - co es - plen - dor,

for the blue - ness of the sky, for the great - ness
für des ho - hen Him - mels Blau, für das gros - se
pour l'a - zur du fir - ma - ment, pour l'im - men - si -
por el cie - lo tan a - zul, por el mar y

of the sea; Praise the Lord, praise the Lord,
wei - te Meer. Lobt unsern Gott, lobt unsern Gott,
té des mers; Lou - ez Dieu, lou - ez Dieu
su vi - gor; A - la - bad al Se - ñor

now and for - ev - er.
jetzt und für al - le - zeit!
main - te - nant, à ja - mais.
a - ho - ra y siem - pre.

Thanks to God,/ Thanks to God, / For the gift of friends in Christ,/ For the church, our house of faith,/ For the gift of wondrous love,/ For the gift of endless grace;/ Thanks to God,/ Thanks to God,/ Now and forever.

Glory to God,/ Glory to God,/ For the grace of Christ, the Son,/ For the love of parent God,/ For the comfort and the strength/ Of the Spirit, Holy God;/ Glory to God,/ Glory to God,/ Now and forever.

Dankt unserm Gott,/ dankt unserm Gott:/ Für die Freundschaft, die Christus schenkt,/ für die Kirche, die uns eint,/ Liebe, die uns staunen läßt,/ Gnade, die sich nie erschöpft;/ dankt unserm Gott,/ dankt unserm Gott,/ jetzt und für allezeit!

Ehre sei Gott,/ Ehre sei Gott:/ Für die Gnade Christi, des Sohns,/ für die Elternliebe aus Gott,/ für den Zuspruch und die Kraft,/ die der heil'ge Geist uns bringt;/ Ehre sei Gott,/ Ehre sei Gott,/ jetzt und für allezeit!

Louez Dieu,/ louez Dieu/ pour le don de l'amitié./ Pour l'Eglise, pour la foi,/ L'émerveillement, l'amour,/ pour la grâce infinie;/ Louez Dieu,/ louez Dieu,/ maintenant, à jamais.

Louez Dieu,/ louez Dieu/ pour la grâce de Jésus-Christ,/ Pour l'amour de Dieu le Père,/ Pour l'Esprit consolateur,/ Pour sa force./ Dieu est saint;/ Louez Dieu,/ louez Dieu,/ maintenant, à jamais.

Gracias dad/ al Señor/ por el don de la amistad,/ por la Iglesia, por la fe,/ por los dones que nos dio,/ por su gracia, por su amor./ Gracias dad/ al Señor/ ahora y siempre.

Gloria a Dios,/ gloria a Dios/ por la gracia de Jesus,/ el amor del Creador,/ el consuelo y el poder/ del Espíritu de Dios./ Gloria a Dios,/ gloria a Dios/ ahora y siempre.

Ephesians 5:20   Tahitian melody   **34**

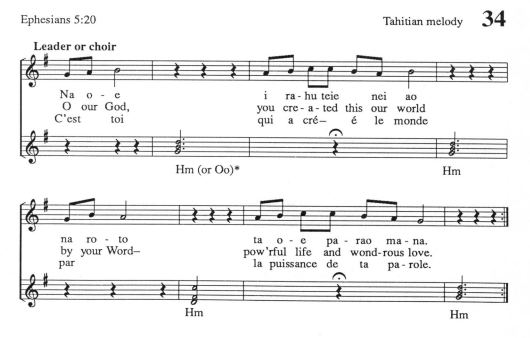

Leader or choir

Na o - e   i ra - hu teie   nei ao
O our God,   you cre - a - ted this our world
C'est toi   qui a cré— é le monde

Hm (or Oo)*   Hm

na ro - to   ta o - e pa - rao ma - na.
by your Word—   pow'rful life and wond-rous love.
par   la puissance de ta pa - role.

Hm   Hm

*expression of "yes" or "I agree."

35 Isaiah 65:17-25   Lois C. Kroehler: Cuba

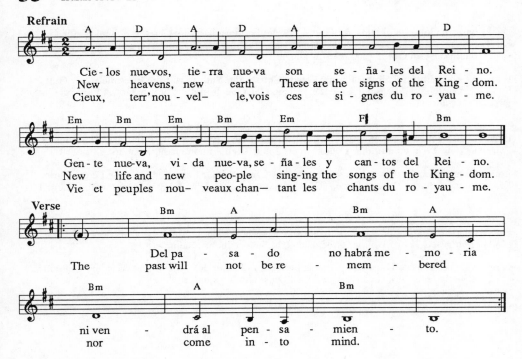

2. Ale- | gría en | la ciu- | dad, | y gran | gozo en el | pueblo.

3. No habrá a-| llí más | ni- | ño que | muera de | pocos | días.

4. Ni tam-| poco an- | cia- | no que sus | dí-| as no | cumpla.

5. Edi-| ficarán | ca-| sas y |vivi-| rán en | ellas.

6. Planta-| rán | vi-| ñas y | come-| rán su | fruta.

7. Disfruta-| rán las | obras de sus | manos, | no trabaja-| rán en | vano.

8. El lobo | y el cor-| de-| ro se-| rán apacen-| tados | juntos.

2. (Re)-joicing | in the | ci-| ty, | and great | joy in the | people.

3. There shall be | no more | in-| fants who | die shortly | after | birth.

4. Nor shall | there be | old | folks who | do not | fill out their | days.

5. They | shall build | hou-| ses | and in-| habit | them.

6. They | shall plant | vine-| yards and | eat the | fruit of | them.

7. They shall en-| joy the | works of their | hands; | they shall not | labor in | vain.

8. (The) wolf | and the | lamb | | shall | feed to-| gether.

Michel Scouarnec

Jo Akepsimas: France **36**

Vous qui ploy - ez sous le far - deau, vous qui cher - chez le
You that by bur - dens hard op - pressed ache to be giv - en

vrai re - pos, Ne crai - gnez pas pour vo - tre corps,
space to rest, fear not the powers that hurt and kill,

Ne crai - gnez pas de - vant la mort, Le - vez les yeux vers
love will prove strong - er than all ill. Lift up your eyes to

le Sei - gneur, cri - ez vers lui sans per - dre coeur.
see the Lord, do not lose heart, and trust his word.

2. Vous qui tombez sur le chemin,/ le coeur blessé par les chagrins,

3. Vous qui pleurez dans vos prisons,/ vous qui fuyez votre maison,

4. Vous que la haine a déchirés,/ vous que les hommes ont crucifiés,

2. You that keep stumbling on life's way,/ empty of heart, with minds afraid,

3. You that in prison cry alone,/ carried away from hearth and home,

4. You, torn apart by human hate,/ you whom the world has crucified,

37 Jaci Maraschin Marcílio de Oliveira Filho: Brazil

Vem, Je - sus nos - sa es - pe - ran - ça, nos - sas vi - das li - ber-
Tú Je - sús, nues - tra es - pe - ran - za, ven y li - bra nues - tro
Come to be our hope, oh Je - sus, come to set our peo - ple

tar. Vem, nas - cer em nós, cri - an - ça, vem o
ser. Ni - ño na - ce en - tre no - so - tros, ven y
free. From op - pres - sion come, re - lease us, let us

teu po - der nos dar. Vem, li - ber - ta os pri - sio-
da - nos tu po - der. Ven, li - bra los pri - sio-
turn to life in Thee. Come, re - lease from e - very

2. Vem tecer um mundo novo/ nos caminhos da verdade;/ para que, afinal, o povo/ viva em plena liberdade./ Vem, Jesus, abre o futuro/ do teu reino de alegria./ Vem, derruba o imenso muro/ que separa a noite e o dia.

2. Ven, y teje un mundo nuevo/ caminando en la verdad,/ para que, por fin, el pueblo/ viva en plena libertad./ Ven, Jesús, abre el futuro/ de tu Reino de alegría./ Ven, derrumba este gran muro/ que hoy separa noche y día.

2. Come to build your new creation/ through the road of servanthood;/ give new life to every nation,/ changing evil into good./ Come and open our tomorrow/ for a Kingdom, now, so near./ Take away all human sorrow,/ give us hope against our fear.

38 Douglas Clark: USA

Lynda Katsuno: Canada

Hope for the child - ren in our midst, Fac - ing a world that's
Hoff - nung für Kin - der un - ter uns, die ei - ne Welt voll
Con es - pe - ran - za en la ni - ñez, to - do con - flic - to

con - flict torn. All that they ask is time to grow, And live the years for
Strei - ten sehn: sie wol - len doch nur Zeit, zu wachsen und Zeit, das Le - ben
se en - fren - ta - rá, a - sí de - je - mos - les cre - cer y vi— vir con

Refrain

which they're born. Hope for the child - ren ev - ery - where.
zu be - stehn. Hoff - nung für Kin - der ü - ber - all.
i - lu - sión. Con es - pe - ran - za en la ni - ñez

We'll build with them a world of peace.
Wir baun mit ih - nen die Welt des Friedens.
cons - tru - i - re - mos un mun - do de paz.

2. Rumours of war sound everywhere,/ wondering if there's chance for peace./ Yet for all children that we love,/ we will not yield 'til hate shall cease.

3. Peace is the goal of all we do./ Love leads to justice on the earth,/ Let justice flow like waters clear,/ so may we see the world's rebirth.

4. Hope for the children yet to be./ Pray they may find years free from war./ Let us make plowshares of all swords,/ harvesting life healed evermore.

2. Reden vom Krieg sind laut zu hörn./ Ob es jemals Frieden gibt?/ Doch für die Kinder, die wir lieben/ weichen wir nicht bis die Liebe siegt.

3. Frieden ist Ziel all unsren Tuns,/ Liebe führt uns zur Gerechtigkeit/ sie wird wie klare Wasser sein,/ Gerechtigkeit und Neubeginn.

4. Für alle, die noch nicht geborn,/ Hoffnung, daß sie den Frieden sehn/ Pflüge sollt ihr aus Schwertern machen/ und euer Leben wird geheilt.

2. Guerras y muerte por doquier,/ ¿Habrá oportunidad de paz?/ A nuestros niños hay que amar/ para que el odio cese ya.

3. Paz es la meta que alcanzar/ y la justicia así mostrar;/ Que como rico manantial/ el mundo venga a renacer.

4. La esperanza en la niñez/ es encontrar un mundo feliz./ Dejen las armas de existir/ y haya en el mundo siempre paz.

Miriam Therese Winter: USA
Luke 1:46b-55

Morning Song **39**

My soul gives glo - ry   to the   Lord.   My heart pours out its
Von gan - zer See - le lob - sin - ge ich Gott, mein Geist ist hoch er -
Mon â - me rend gloire   au Sei - gneur. Mon coeur chante et le

praise. God   lif - ted   up my   low - li - ness in man - y mar-ve-lous ways.
freut. Denn er hob mich em-por aus Nied-rig - keit, ein Ret-ter, der   mich liebt.
loue. Dieu   a   vu   mon hu - mi - li - té. Il m'a   re - le - vée.

2. My God has done great things for me:/ yes, holy is this name./ All people will declare me blessed,/ and blessings they shall claim.

3. From age to age, to all who fear,/ such mercy love imparts,/ dispensing justice far and near,/ dismissing selfish hearts.

4. Love casts the mighty from their thrones,/ promotes the insecure,/ leaves hungry spirits satisfied,/ the rich seem suddenly poor.

5. Praise God, whose loving covenant/ supports those in distress,/ remembering past promises/ with present faithfulness.

2. Für mich hat Gott große Dinge getan,/ sein Name heilig heißt./ Selig wird mich nun preisen alles Volk,/ um Segen wird es flehn.

3. Zu aller Zeit wird, wer Gott fürchtet, sehn,/ wie Gnade Liebe schenkt,/ wie Gerechtigkeit wächst für fern und nah,/ wie Ichsucht Herzen flieht.

4. Die Liebe schleudert die Starken vom Thron/ und richtet Schwache auf,/ und den Hungernden gibt sie täglich Brot,/ läßt Reiche leer ausgehn.

5. Es bleibt Gott treu seinem Volk Israel,/ erbarmt sich seiner Not/ und vergißt nicht, was er ihm einst versprach,/ dem Samen Abrahams.

2. Le Seigneur Dieu est merveilleux./ Saint, Saint est son nom./ Tout le peuple me dit bénie,/ bénédiction sur lui.

3. D'âge en âge pour celui qui craint et de Dieu/ reçoit l'amour/ la justice abonde. Elle fait chanter les mondes.

4. L'Amour détrône les puissants,/ rend l'humble confiant,/ satisfait l'esprit affamé./ Le riche est renvoyé.

5. Fidèle est le Dieu d'Israël,/ écoutant nos prières,/ se souvenant de ses promesses,/ pour Abr'am et ses enfants.

40   South Africa

Siph' a - man - dla Nko - si. Wo - kung - e - sa - bi. Siph'
O God give us pow - er to rip down pri - sons. O
O Gott gib uns Stär - ke, dass Ket - ten sprin - gen. O
O Sei - gneur, don - ne - nous ta puis - san - ce pour O
Di - os, da - nos fuer - za bo - tar pri - sio - nes. Di -

a - man - dla Nko - si. Si - ya - wa - ding - a.
God give us pow - er to lift the peo - ple.
Gott, gib uns Stär - ke, dass wir auf - ste - hen.
dé - truire les pri - sons ai - der les peu - ples.
os da - nos fuer - za al - zar al pueb - lo.

2. O God give us courage/ To withstand hatred./ O God give us courage/ Not to be bitter.

3. O God give us power/ And make us fearless./ O God give us power/ Because we need it.

2. O Gott gib uns Hoffnung,/ dem Hass zu wehren/ O Gott, gib uns Hoffnung,/ nicht zu verbittern.

3. O Gott gib uns Stärke,/ und mach uns furchtlos/ O Gott, gib uns Stärke/ weil wir sie brauchen.

2. O Seigneur, donne-nous/ ton courage/ pour vaincre la haine/ et l'amertume.

3. O Seigneur, donne-nous/ ta puissance/ pour être sans faiblesse/ Viens-nous en aide.

2. Dios, danos fuerza/ andar sin miedo./ Dios, danos fuerza/ te lo pedimos.

The Iona Community: United Kingdom   Praise my soul (J. Goss) **41**

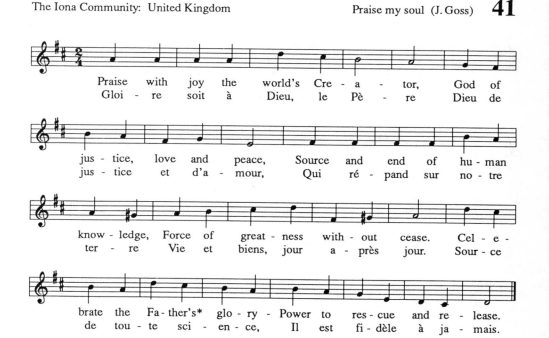

Praise   with   joy   the   world's   Cre - a - tor,   God   of
Gloi - re   soit   à   Dieu,   le   Pè - re   Dieu   de

jus - tice,   love   and   peace,   Source   and   end   of   hu - man
jus - tice   et   d'a - mour,   Qui   ré - pand   sur   no - tre

know - ledge,   Force   of   great - ness   with - out   cease.   Cel - e -
ter - re   Vie   et   biens,   jour   a - près   jour.   Sour - ce

brate   the   Fa - ther's*   glo - ry - Power   to   res - cue   and   re - lease.
de   tou - te   sci - en - ce,   Il   est   fi - dèle   à   ja - mais.

2. Praise the Son who feeds the hungry,/ Frees the captive, finds the lost,/ Heals the sick, upsets religion,/ Fearless both of fate and cost./ Celebrate Christ's constant presence--/ Friend and Stranger, Guest and Host.

3. Praise the Spirit sent among us,/ Liberating truth from pride,/ Forging bonds where race or gender,/ Age or nation dare divide./ Celebrate the Spirit's treasure--/ Foolishness none dare deride.

4. Praise the Father*, Son and Spirit,/ One God in Community,/ Calling Christians to embody/ Oneness and diversity./ Thus the world shall yet believe when/ shown Christ's vibrant unity.

*Originally Maker

2. Gloire au Fils qui nous libère/ De la faim, de nos prisons,/ Retrouve celui qui erre/ Et l'accueille en sa maison./ Sa présence nous fait vivre/ Et donne la guérison.

3. Gloire à l'Esprit qui rassemble/ Tous les hommes dispersés,/ Leur apprend à vivre ensemble/ Divers dans leur unité./ Corps du Christ, signe des cieux,/ Promesse d'un monde heureux!

4. Gloire soit à Dieu le Père./ Le Fils et le Saint-Esprit,/ Un seul Dieu qui, sur la terre/ Nous appelle et nous bénit,/ Pour que l'unité vivante/ Soit pour tout homme un espoir!

42 Psalms 85:10 Myra Blyth: United Kingdom

Let us hear! Let us hear what God the Lord has
Hö - ren wir, hö - ren wir, was Gott, der Herr, uns
E - cou - tons! E - cou - tons la Pa - ro - le du Sei -
Es - cu - che - mos, es - cu - che - mos la Pa - la - bra del Se -

said: Jus - tice and peace em - brace one an - oth - er. Jus - tice and
sagt: Ge - rech - tig - keit soll Frie - den brin - gen. Frie - den, Ge -
gneur: jus - tice et paix se ren - con - tre - ront, jus - tice et
ñor: Jus - ti - cia y paz se han a - bra - za - do. Jus - ti - cia y

peace em - brace one an - oth - er.
rech - tig - keit um - ar - men sich.
paix bien - tôt s'em - bras - se - ront.
paz se han a - bra - za - do.

43 Zoito Yanapa Chambi: Bolivia-Aymara

Carnavalito

Dm   B♭   C7   F

Ta - ta - na - ka ma - ma - na - ka sa - ran - ta - ña - ni!
Let the wo - men and the men all move to - geth - er.
Laßt uns ge - hen, laßt uns ge - hen, Schwes - tern und Brü - der.
Ca - mi - ne - mos las mu - je - res y los hom - bres.

Gm   A7   Dm

Way - na - na - ca, tawa - ko - na - ca, say - ta - si - ña - ni.
Let the chil - dren and the youth come close to - geth - er.
Laßt uns fest zu - sam - men - stehn, zu - sam - men ge - hen.
Y los jó - ve - nes lu - che - mos siem - pre fir - mes.

Ernesto B. Cardoso, Paulo Roberto, Déa Affini
Eder Soares, Tércio Junker and Darlene: Brazil

44

Marcha-Rancho

Deus cha- ma a gen - te pra'um mo-men - to no - vo de ca- mi -
Dios hoy nos lla-ma a un mo-men - to nue - vo, a ca- mi -
God calls his peo - ple now to a new life walk-ing a -

nhar jun - to com seu po - vo. E ho - ra de trans-for - mar o
nar jun - to con su pue - blo. Es ho - ra de trans-for - mar lo
long to-geth - er hand in hand; The time is ripe for chang–ing, the

que não dá mais: so zi - nho i - so - la - do, nin - guém é ca-paz. Por is - so,
que no da más, y so - lo y ais-la - do no hay na - die ca-paz. Por e - so
mo-ment is now. Let's walk to-geth-er: no one can go a-lone! So, come and

v'em! En - tra na ro - da com a gen - te tam bém!
ven, en - tra a la rue - da con to - dos, tam - bién
join! Get in a cir - cle with all the peo - ple. Come!

Vo - cê é mui - to im-por tan - te, por is - so, tan- te! Vem!
tu e - res muy im-por tan - te, por e - so, tan- te! Ven!
Your hands and hearts are im - por-tant, so come and por-tant! Come!

2. Não é possível crer que tudo é fácil,/ há muita força que produz a morte,/ gerando dor, tristeza e desolação./ E necessário unir o cordão.

3. A força que hoje faz brotar a vida/ atua em nós pela sua graça./ É Deus que nos convida pra trabalhar,/ o amor repartir e as forças juntar.

2. Ya no es posible creer que todo es fácil,/ hay muchas fuerzas que producen muerte,/ nos dan dolor, tristeza y desolación,/ es necesario afianzar nuestra unión.

3. La fuerza que hace hoy brotar la vida/ obra en nosotros dándonos su gracia;/ es Dios que nos convida a trabajar,/ su amor repartir y las fuerzas juntar.

2. We must not think that things are always easy,/ while wicked people cause suff'ring and death,/ and many others don't seem to care at all./ Let's walk together: no one can go alone!

3. The power today that makes new life burst forth/ is now in us through the gift of grace./ It's God who calls us to work together for justice./ Let's walk together: no one can go alone!

45 Uwe Seidel

Fritz Baltruweit: Germany

Gib mir dei - ne Hand. Wan-drer durch die Zei-ten, gib mir dei - ne
Give me your hand, Let us be for - ev - er, on the life-long
Don-ne-moi la main, que nous so - yons tou-jours sur le long che-
Da - me tu ma-no, e - ter - no ca - mi - nan-te, da - me tu

Hand, lass mich dich be - glei - ten. Gib mir dei - ne Hand,
path, Com-pan-ions, now to - geth - er. Give me your hand,
min, Com - pa - gnons, dans la vi - e. Don-ne-moi la main,
ma-no, quie ro a - com - pa - ñar - te. Da - me tu ma-no, her-

Schwes - ter auf un - ser-en We-gen. Gib mir dei - ne Hand,
Sis - ter wher-ev - er we tra-vel, Give me your hand
ma soeur dans le vo - ya-ge. Don-ne-moi la main,
ma - na en nues-tro ca - mi-no Da - me tu ma-no, her-

Bru - der auf schma - len Ste - gen. Gib mir dei - ne Hand, lass uns
Bro - ther on nar - row path-ways, Give me your hand, let us
frè - re du che - min é - troit. Don-ne-moi la main, res - tons
ma - no en el pe - li - gro. Da - me tu ma-no, mar-

fest zu-sam-men - stehn und da - hin gehn, wo Frie-den wohnt, und
stead-fast be in love. And move to-wards where peace a - bides and
frè - res dans l'a - mour. A - van - çons vers la paix, a - van - çons
che - mos bien u - ni - dos has-ta al-can zar a com-tem - plar y

da - hin gehn, wo Frie - den wohnt. Gib uns dei - ne
move to - wards where peace a - bides. Give us your
là où la paix de - meu - re. Don - ne - nous la
com - par - tir con to - dos la paz. Da - nos tu

Hand, mein Gott. Schüt-ze uns-re See - len, da-mit wir nicht
hand, O God, Guide us in our liv - ing, Grant us your for-
main, O Dieu, ac-cor-de-nous la vie. Ac-cor-de-nous
ma-no o Dios, y pro-te-ge nues tro an-dar no nos de-jes

feh - len, gib uns dei - ne Hand.
giv - ing. Give us your hand.
ton par - don. Don - ne - nous la main.
tro - pe - zar, Da - nos tu ma - no o Dios.

Jacques Berthier: Taizé, France   **46**

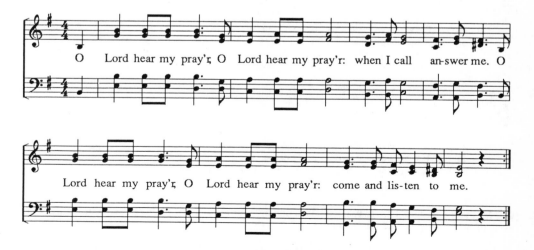

O Lord hear my pray'r, O Lord hear my pray'r: when I call an-swer me. O

Lord hear my pray'r, O Lord hear my pray'r: come and lis-ten to me.

Gott, hör mein Gebet! Rufe ich, antworte! Gott, hör mein Gebet, komm und höre mich an!

47 Jonas Jonson

Per Harling: Sweden

Refrain

Där Guds An - de är, är fri - het.
Where the Spir - it is theres free-dom.
Wo der Geist wohnt, da ist Frei-heit.
Là où est l'Es - prit, li - ber - té!

Där Guds An - de är, där är liv.
Where the Spir - it is, there is life!
Wo der Geist wohnt, da ist Le - ben.
Là où est l'Es - prit, vi - vez!

Verse

In - te av värl - den kan fri - he - ten nä - ras in - te av ting
Not by the world can our free-dom be nour-ished, not by our things,
Nicht von der Welt kann die Frei-heit le - ben, nicht von Sa - chen,
Non pas com - me le mon - de la don - ne. Mais, nour - ri - e

en - dast av An - de. Ö - va er barn att le - va i An - den
on - ly by Spir - it. Prac - tice my chil-dren to live by the Spir - it,
sie lebt nur vom Geist. Lernt mei - ne Kin-der, im Geis - te zu le - ben,
Par l'Es - prit. Vi - vez, mes en - fants, la vie de l'Es-prit,

läm - na er roll klä er i fri - het!
drop all your masks, take free-dom's cloth - ing!
legt Mas - ken ab, zieht Frei - heit an!
plus de masques, en Christ la li - ber - té

2. Himmel på jorden/ här får vi leva/ älska och ge/ burna av glädje./ Öva er barn/ att leva i Anden/ våga idag/ smaka Guds framtid.

3. Såren kan läkas/ maskerna faller/ mänska av Gud/ avspeglar Kristus./ Öva er barn/ att leva i Anden/ himlen är här/ evig i tiden.

2. Kingdom of God,/ present among us,/ gives to us all/ strength for the journey./ Practise my children to live by the Spirit,/ tasting today hope of God's future!

3. Wounds will be healed,/ eyes will be opened,/ imaging God,/ reflecting Jesus,/ practice my children to live by the Spirit,/ heaven is here,/ time made eternal!

2. Himmel auf Erden,/ hier wo wir wohnen,/ teilen die Gaben,/ freudig gebracht./ Lernt meine Kinder, im Geiste zu leben/ spürt heute schon,/ Hoffnung und Zukunft.

3. Wunden verheilen,/ wir sehen plötzlich/ Gottes Gesicht/ in Jesus an./ Lernt meine Kinder, im Geiste zu leben/ Himmel ist hier,/ Zeit dauert ewig.

2. Le ciel a visité notre terre,/ Partage et joie/ De tous les dons./ Vivez, mes enfants, la vie de l'Esprit,/ Goûtez l'espoir en Christ/ est l'avenir

3. Toutes nos plaies et nos meurtrissures/ Nos yeux verront/ la guérison./ Vivez, mes enfants, la vie de l'Esprit,/ Car ici-bas commence,/ l'éternité.

Lynda Katsuno: Canada   **48**

From the Spir-it have we all re - ceived, grace up-on grace.
Durch den Geist ha-ben wir al-le emp-fangen Gna-de um Gnade.
Re-çue de Dieu, Sa grâce nous a com-blés, in-fi-ni-ment.
El Es-pí-ri-tu a to-dos nos dió, gra-cia sin fin.

49 Bahram Dehqani and Bishop Hassan Dehqani: Iran

With quiet majesty

You, oh my God, gifts of know - ledge give to me,
Da - me, mi Dios, do - nes pa - ra com - pren - der;

that hid - den mys - ter - ies I may clear - ly see.
que los mis - te - ri - os pue - da clara - mente ver.

Free me from in - ward fights, life's tang - led skein.
Lí - bra - me de an - sie - dad y con - fu - sión,

My torn heart heal, oh Lord, make me glad a - gain.
sa - na mi co - ra - zón con tu go - zo y paz.

Bahram was the only son of Bishop and Mrs. Dehqani-Tafti. He composed this song before he was martyred in Iran on May 6th, 1980.

2. Spirit of God, Source of wisdom, guidance, life,/ Yet to receive these gifts, we must daily die./ Spirit of Jesus Christ reaches our pain,/ Consciences weak through guilt, He'll make whole again.

3. Love from the human heart through selfishness will fail,/ love that Your Spirit gives, causes it to pale./ Lord fill us deep within, so friends will know,/ to even enemies, Your love we can show.

4. Jesus, we'll follow You, servant hearts we need,/ with Your compassion, Lord, others we will feed./ Grant us to follow You, never retreat,/ gladly to wash and cleanse one another's feet.

5. People without God are living for themselves,/ bringing such sep'rateness, suffering and fear./ Come Lord and show us all Your power can heal,/ uproot the source of hate, may Your peace reign here.

6. You, oh my God, gifts of knowledge give to me/ that hidden mysteries I may clearly see./ Living obediently, grace You'll endue,/ my soul and character You'll make wholly new.

2. Para poder tus favores recibir/ debemos cada día junto a ti morir,/ y por tu Espíritu al corazón/ herido por el mal restaurarás.

3. Si nuestro amor es un débil resplandor/ que empalidece junto a tu propio fulgor,/ danos, Señor, poder para mostrar/ que a amigos y enemigos podemos amar.

4. Te seguiremos, Jesús, de corazón,/ sirviendo a todos con tu misma compasión;/ con humildad, Señor, para lavar/ los pies de aquel que tú nos pediste amar.

5. Sin Dios, la gente se cierra sobre sí,/ aislada por poderes que la hacen sufrir./ Muéstranos, oh Señor, que tu poder/ al odio y al terror puede hoy vencer.

6. Dame, oh Dios, dones para comprender;/ que los misterios pueda claramente ver./ Voy a aceptar con fe tu voluntad/ para que así mi ser puedas renovar.

50   Shirley Murray: Aoteroa/New Zealand   I-to Loh: Taiwan

Lov - ing Spir - it,   lov - ing Spir - it,   you have cho - sen
Geist der Lie - be,   Geist der Lie - be,   du hast mich ins
Es - prit de Dieu   ad - mi - ra - ble.   Tu m'as choi - si(e),

me   to   be.   You have drawn me   to   your won - der,
Le-ben ge-bracht.   Du hast mich ins   Licht   ge - zo - gen,
en - voie-moi.   Tu m'at - ti - res,   tu   me con - duis

you   have   set   your   sign   on   me.
hast   mich   dir   zu   ei - gen   ge - macht.
vers   la   beau - té   de   tes   lois.

2. Like a mother, you enfold me,/ hold my life within your own,/ feed me with your very body,/ form me of your flesh and bone.

3. Like a father, you protect me,/ teach me the discerning eye,/ hoist me up upon your shoulder,/ let me see the world from high.

4. Friend and lover, in your closeness/ I am known and held and blessed:/ in your promise is my comfort,/ in your presence I may rest.

5. Loving Spirit, loving Spirit,/ you have chosen me to be/ you have drawn me to your wonder,/ you have set your sign on me.

2. Mütterlich hältst du mich umfangen/ halt' mich an dir, Tag und Nacht,/ sei du selbst mir Kraft und Speise./ Ich bin ja von dir gemacht.

3. Wie ein Vater, schützt du mich täglich,/ gib mir Weitsicht und Verstand,/ nimm mich hoch auf deine Schulter/ laß von dort mich sehn Stadt und Land.

4. Freundschaftlich und voller Liebe/ kennst du mich und bist mir nah./ Trost und Segen find' ich bei dir./ Wo du bist, ist Frieden da.

5. Geist der Liebe, Geist der Liebe,/ du hast mich ins Leben gebracht,/ du hast mich ins Licht gezogen,/ hast mich dir zu eigen gemacht.

2. Comm' une mère tu m'entoures/ Tenant ma vie dans tes mains,/ Tu m'as formé(e) comme ton corps,/ Tu m'as nourri(e) de ton pain.

3. Comm' un père tu me gardes,/ Enseigne-moi à aimer/ La justice venant de toi,/ En tout lieu la contempler.

4. Ami aimé, auprès de toi/ Je suis chéri(e) et béni(e),/ Mon réconfort, ma promesse,/ C'est en toi que je revis.

5. Esprit de Dieu admirable/ Tu m'as choisi(e), envoie-moi!/ Tu m'attires, tu me conduis/ Vers la beauté de tes lois.

51   Gordon Light: Canada

Refrain

She comes sail - ing on the wind, her wings flash-ing in the sun; on a
Sie kommt se - gelnd mit dem Wind, in der Son - ne leuch-tet sie, ih - re
Sur ses ai - les dé - ploy - ées au - ré - o - lées de so - leil el - le

jour - ney just be - gun, she flies on. And in the pas - sage of her
Rei - se nimmt sie auf durch die Welt. Und ihr Ge - sang tönt in der
prend son en - vo - lée dans le vent. Et au sein de l'obs - cu - ri -

flight, her song rings out thro' the night, full of laugh - ter, full of
Nacht, Licht und La - chen bringt sie mit, auf der Rei - se, die be -
té son chant fait vi - brer la nuit plein de ri - res et de lu -

Verse

light, she flies on. Si - lent wat - ers rock - ing on the
ginnt durch die Welt. Wie die lee - re Wie - ge war - tet
mière dans le vent. Et les eaux se ber - cent à l'au -

morn - ing of our birth, like an emp - ty cra - dle wait - ing to be
auf un - sre Ge - burt, wie die ru - hige Wo - ge schau - kelt auf dem
be du pre - mier jour com - me un ber - ceau vide pa - ré pour la

filled, to be filled. And from the heart of God the Spir - it moved up - on the
Meer; und wie bei ei - ner Mut - ter, die dem Kind das Le - ben
vie, pour la vie. Et du coeur de Dieu l'Es - prit se ré - pand sur la terre en -

earth, like a moth - er breath - ing life in - to her child.
schenkt, kam der Geist aus Got - tes Her - zen in die Welt.
tière u - ne mè - re souf - flant vie dans son en - fant.

2. Many were the dreamers whose eyes were given sight,/ When the Spirit filled their dreams with life and form./ The deserts turned to gardens, broken hearts found new delight,/ And then down the ages still she flew on.

3. (To a) gentle girl from Galilee, a gentle breeze she came,/ A whisper softly calling in the dark,/ The promise of a child of Peace, whose reign would never end,/ Mary sang the Spirit song within her heart.

4. Flying to the river, She waited circling high,/ A-bove the child now grown so full of grace./ As he rose up from the water, She swept down from the sky,/ And She carried him away in her embrace.

5. (Long) after the deep darkness, that fell upon the world,/ After dawn return'd in flame of rising sun./ The Spirit touched the earth again, again her wings unfurled,/ Bringing life in wind and fire as She flew on.

2. Viele Menschen sahen in ihren Träumen Leid und Licht/ die der Geist erhellte in der Dunkelheit./ Wüsten wurden Gärten, Menschen fanden neues Glück,/ durch die Zeiten setzt sie ihre Reise fort.

3. Wie ein leises Flüstern in der Nacht,/ berührt von Zärtlichkeit,/ nahm Maria ihren Sohn in sich auf;/ als ein Kind des Friedens,/ Gottes stete Gegenwart,/ schließt das Lied des Geistes in ihr Herz sie ein.

2. Nombreux sont les rêveurs/ qui ont retrouvé leur vie/ quand l'Esprit aux rêves donna forme et vie./ Les déserts sont refleuris, les coeurs brisés retrouvent joie./ La colombe reprend son vol dans le temps.

3. Et la douce brise/ caressa la jeune fille/ un murmure dans la nuit de son destin./ Une promesse de paix dans un enfant au règne sans fin./ Et le coeur de Marie déborda de chants.

4. La blanche colombe/ vers le Jourdain prit son vol/ et plana sur le jeune homme plein de grâce/ et descendit sur lui qui sortait de l'eau de son baptême/ et l'entoura de son souffle tout puissant.

5. Vint la nuit obscure/ qui enveloppa la terre/ et puis l'aube en feu du soleil du matin/ à nouveau l'Esprit toucha la terra ailes déployées/ apportant vie par le feu et par le vent.Å

52

Ev - lo - gi - tos i Chri - ste o The - os i—
O bless - ed are———— You, O Christ Our—
O bé - ni sois———— Tu, O Christ No - tre

mon o pan - so— fus tus a - li - is a - na - thi - xas
God. Who by send- ing down the Ho - ly Spir - it up - on them
Dieu. Qui en en - vo - yant Ton Es - prit Saint——— sur eux

ka - ta - pem - psas af - tis to pnev - ma to a—
made the fish - er - men wise and through them il - lu -
les fit pê - cheurs d'hom- mes et par eux il - lu - mi - na

gi— on ke thi af - ton tin i - ku - me - nin sa - gi - nef -
mined the world and to You the u - ni - verse was ev - er drawn -
le monde et vers Toi tout l'u - ni - vers fut at - ti - ré—

sas fi - lan - thro - pe tho - xa Si.
all glo - ry to You O Lord.
Gloire à Toi, Gloire à Toi Sei - gneur.

Anna-Maija Raittila

Ilkka Kuusisto: Finland **53**

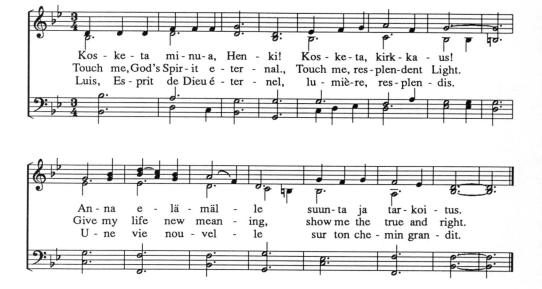

Kos - ke - ta mi - nu - a, Hen - ki! Kos - ke - ta, kirk - ka - us!
Touch me, God's Spir - it e - ter - nal., Touch me, res - plen-dent Light.
Luis, Es - prit de Dieu é - ter - nel, lu - miè-re, res - plen - dis.

An - na e - lä - mäl - le suun-ta ja tar - koi - tus.
Give my life new mean - ing, show me the true and right.
U - ne vie nou - vel - le sur ton che - min gran - dit.

2. Kosketa, Jumalan Henki,/ syvälle sydämeen./ Sinne paina hiljaa/ luottamus Jeesukseen.

3. Rohkaise minua, Henki,/ murenna pelkoni./ Tässä maailmassa/ osoita paikkani.

4. Valaise, Jumalan Henki,/ silmäni aukaise,/ että voisin olla/ ystävä toisille.

5. Kosketa minua, Henki!/ Herätä kiittämään,/ sinun lähelläsi/ armosta elämään.

2. Touch me, God's Spirit, and soothe me/ Deep in my restless soul./ Give me trust in Jesus./ Heal me and make me whole.

3. Spirit of God, give me courage,/ Banish my doubts and fears./ Show me my vocation/ Through all my days and years.

4. Spirit of God, brightly shining,/ Open my eyes to see/ Those who need my friendship:/ Join us in unity.

5. Touch me, God's Spirit eternal./ Teach me to thank and praise./ By your grace be near me,/ Guide me in all my ways.

2. Luis, Esprit de Dieu apaisant/ Calme mon âme/ en Jésus tout repose/ Ta paix émane.

3. Esprit de Dieu tu nous conduis/ Tu encourages/ Toutes les vocations/ Dans tous les âges.

4. Esprit de Dieu, tu resplendis/ ouvre mes yeux pour voir/ ceux qui sur notre route/ Ont besoin d'espoir.

5. Luis en moi, Esprit Eternel/ Que te chante ma voix/ Que ta suprême grâce/ Me guide dans mes voies.

54

Simei Monteiro: Brazil

Tu - a Pa - la - vra na vi - da
E - sa Pa - la - bra en la vi - da
Your word in our lives, e - ter - nal,

é fon - te que ja - mais se - ca,
es fuen - te que no se se - ca,
it is a clear foun - tain flow - ing;

á - gua que a - ni - ma e res - tau - ra
a - gua que a - ni - ma y res - tau - ra
wa - ter that gives strength and cou - rage

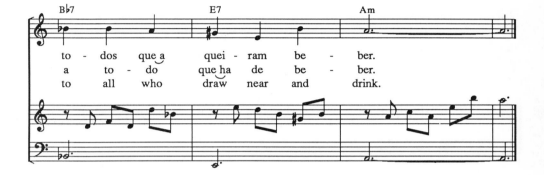

2. Tua Palavra na vida/ é qual semente que brota;/ torna-se bom alimento,/ pão que não há de faltar.

3. Tua Palavra na vida/ é espelho que bem reflete,/ onde nos vemos, sinceros,/ como a imagem de Deus.

4. Tua Palavra na vida/ é espada tão penetrante/ que revelando as verdades/ vai renovando o viver.

5. Tua Palavra na vida/ é luz que os passos clareia,/ para que ao fim no horizonte/ se veja o Reino de Deus.

2. Esa Palabra en la vida/ es cual semilla que brota;/ llega a ser buen alimento/ que no ha jamás de faltar.

3. Esa Palabra en la vida/ espejo es que bien refleja,/ donde nos vemos, sinceros,/ como la imagen de Dios.

4. Esa Palabra en al vida/ espada es tan penetrante/ que revelando verdades/ va renovando el vivir.

5. Esa Palabra en la vida,/ luz que los pasos aclara,/ muestra al final el camino/ del Reino eterno de Dios.

2. Your word in our lives, eternal,/ seed of the Kingdom that's growing;/ it becomes bread for our tables,/ food for the feast without end.

3. Your word in our lives, eternal,/ becomes the mirror where we see/ the true reflection of ourselves:/ children and image of God.

4. Your word in our lives, eternal,/ it is a sharp two-edged sword;/ dividing our lies from your truth,/ it's bringing new life to all.

5. Your word in our lives, eternal,/ is light that shines on the long road/ that leads us to the horizon/ and the bright Kingdom of God.

55 Norman Habel   Robin Mann: Australia

Lift this child to the sun,   Raise this child to the
Hebt dies' Kind hoch zur Sonne, hebt zum Him - mel es
Es - te ni - ño al - za - rás   ha - cia el cie - lo, hacia el

sky;   God has come   from a - bove,   Come to
hoch. Gott kommt zu uns in die Welt,   kommt zur
sol;   ha ve - ni—   do— Dios,   a la

earth   from on high.   Lift this child,   lift this child to the
Er - de her - ab.   Hebt dies' Kind,   hebt dies' Kind hoch zur
tie - rra ba - jó.   Es - te niño   al - za - rás ha-cia el

vs. 1,2,3,4   vs. 5

sun.   night.
Sonne. Nacht.
sol.   ás.

2. Lay this child on the ground,/ One with us, one with earth;/ Let God know in His Son/
Human clay, human birth./ Lay this child, lay this child on the ground.

3. Lay this child in the shade,/ Hang this child 'neath a tree;/ With His hand on the wood/ May
this child set us free./ Place this child, place this child in the shade.

4. Send this child down the road,/ Let Him ride hard the track;/ To be king of the bush/ And the
harsh world outback./ Send this child, send this child down the road.

5. Lift this child to the night,/ To the silence of God;/ Let this child cry for us,/ And the silence
be heard./ Lift this child, lift this child to the night.

2. Legt dies' Kind auf die Erde/ eins mit ihr, eins mit uns/ Gott selbst spürte im Sohn/ Stein und
Menschengeburt/ Legt dies' Kind, legt dies' Kind zur Erde.

3. Setzt dies' Kind in den Schatten/ stellt es neben den Baum/ Holz und Stamm soll es spüren/
und es soll uns befrein/ Setzt dies' Kind, setzt dies' Kind in den Schatten.

4. Schickt dies' Kind auf den Weg/ mitten in Schmutz und Staub/ wird er König im Land/ über
Wüste und Meer/ Schickt dies' Kind, schickt dies' Kind auf den Weg.

5. Schickt dies Kind in die Nacht,/ in die Stille des Herrn/ laßt es rufen für uns/ und die Stille
wird laut/ Schickt dies' Kind, schickt dies' Kind in die Nacht.

2. Este niño de Dios/ en la tierra pondrás;/ es de barro y también/ como tú nacerá./ Este niño en
la tierra pondrás.

3. Este niño estará/ a la sombra fugaz/ del y árbol que él hará/ signo de libertad./ Este niño a la
sombra pondrás.

4. Este niño enviarás,/ por caminos que van/ hacia el duro trajín/ de este mundo sin paz./ Este
niño por el mundo enviarás.

5. Este niño alzarás/ hacia la oscuridad,/ y el silencio de Dios/ en su voz nos oirá./ Este niño,
este niño alzarás.

John 1: 29   Rolf Schweizer: Germany **56**

Sie - he,   das ist   Got - tes Lamm,   das   der   Welt Sün - de   trägt.
Look, the   Lamb of   God, who takes   sin   a - way from the   world.
Re - gard - ez, l'agn - eau de Dieu,   qui en - lève le pé - ché du   monde.

57 Aboriginal people of Arnhem Land   Aboriginal: Australia
        versified by D'Arcy Wood

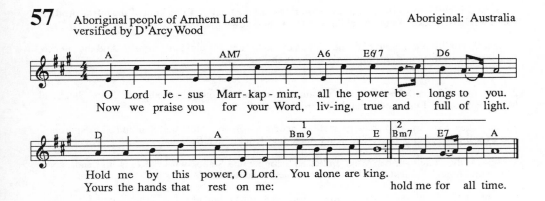

O Lord Je - sus Marr - kap - mirr, all the power be - longs to you.
Now we praise you   for your Word, liv - ing, true and full of light.

Hold me by this power, O Lord. You alone are king.
Yours the hands that   rest on me: hold me for all time.

Marrkapmirr is a term of endearment, and means in this context 'altogether lovely, and worthy of affection'.

58   India

Ja - gat pi - ta - ve, Ja - ya ja - ya te. Ja - ya ja - ya rak sha Kan

I - sa su - ta. Ja - ya ja - ya pa - ve - ne pa - vit - rat - ma - ve.

Father of the universe, Saviour of our souls, praise be to You!
Vater des Universums, Retter unserer Seelen, gepriesen seist Du.
Père de l'univers, Sauveur de nos âmes, gloire à Toi.
Padre del universo, Salvador de nuestras almas, ¡Te alabamos!

Jacques Berthier: Taizé, France **59**

Let nothing trouble you, let nothing frighten you: whoever has God lacks nothing. God alone is enough.

Nichts beunruhige dich, nichts ängstige dich: Wer Gott hat, dem fehlt nichts. Gott allein genügt.

Que rien ne te trouble, rien ne t'effraie: qui a Dieu ne manque de rien. Seul Dieu suffit.

60 Psalm 137:1 Anonymous

By the wa - ters, the wa - ters of Ba - by - lon
An den Was - sern, den Was - sern von Ba - by - lon
Sur les ri - ves, sur les ri - ves, sur les riv' de Ba - by - lone
Jun - to a los rí - os de Ba - bi - lo - nia nos so - lí - a - mos mos sen - tar

we lay down and wept, and wept for you Zi - on: we re - mem - ber,
sas - sen wir und wein - ten, und wein - ten, um Dich Zi - on, nie ver - ges - sen,
nous a - vons pleu - ré pleu - ré pour toi, Si - on: t'en sou - viens - tu?
y a - cor - dán - do - nos de Sión. Llo - rá - ba - mos re - cor - dan - do,

we re - mem - ber, we re - mem - ber you Zi - on.
nie ver - ges - sen, nie ver - ges - sen wir Zi - on.
t'en sou - viens - tu? t'en sou - viens - tu Si - on?
re - cor - dan - do, re - cor - dan - do siem - pre a Sión.

As taught by Daisy Nshakazongwe: Botswana **61**

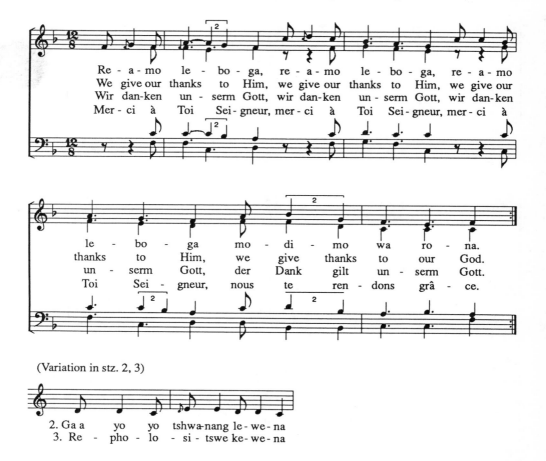

Re - a - mo le - bo - ga, re - a - mo le - bo - ga, re - a - mo
We give our thanks to Him, we give our thanks to Him, we give our
Wir dan-ken un - serm Gott, wir dan-ken un - serm Gott, wir dan-ken
Mer - ci à Toi Sei - gneur, mer - ci à Toi Sei - gneur, mer - ci à

le - bo - ga mo - di - mo wa ro - na.
thanks to Him, we give thanks to our God.
un - serm Gott, der Dank gilt un - serm Gott.
Toi Sei - gneur, nous te ren - dons grâ - ce.

(Variation in stz. 2, 3)

2. Ga a yo yo tshwa-nang le - we - na
3. Re - pho - lo - si - tswe ke - we - na

2. There is no one like Him./ (3x) There's no one like our God.

3. We have been saved by Him./ (3x) We've been saved by our God.

2. Denn Gott ist niemand gleich,/ (3x) niemand gleicht unserm Gott.

3. Wir sind durch Gott befreit./ (3x) befreit durch unsern Gott.

2. Aucun n'est comme Toi./ (3x) Comme Toi, Oh Seigneur.

3. C'est lui qui nous sauva./ (3x) C'est Dieu qui nous sauva.

62 Afro-American Spiritual: USA

Leader / Response

Guide my feet while I run this race.
Leit mei-nen Fuß un-ter-wegs zum Ziel.
Guide mes pas quand je m'é-lan-ce.

yes, my Lord!
Ja, mein Gott!
Oui, Sei-gneur.

Guide my feet while I run this race.
Leit mei-nen Fuß un-ter-wegs zum Ziel.
Guide mes pas quand je m'é-lan-ce.

yes, my Lord!
Ja, mein Gott!
Oui, Sei-gneur.

Guide my feet while I run this race, for I
Leit mei-nen Fuß un-ter-wegs zum Ziel, daß mein
Guide mes pas quand je m'é-lan-ce, car je

don't want to run this race in vain! (race in vain!)
Mü-hen und Lau-fen nicht ver-geb-lich ist! (ver-geb-lich ist!)
ne veux pas cou—rir en vain! (pas en vain!)

2. Hold my hand	2. Halt meine Hand	2. Tiens-moi la main
3. Stand by me	3. Steh mir bei	3. Reste vers moi
4. I'm Your child	4. Ich bin dein Kind	4. Je t'appartiens
5. Search my heart	5. Prüfe mein Herz	5. Cherche mon coeur
6. Guide my feet	6. Leit meinen Fuß	6. Guide mes pas

Church Slavonic   Bulgaria **63**

Mno - ga - ia le - ta, mno - ga - ia le - ta,

mno - ga - ia le ta.

Many years   Viele Jahre   Ad multos annos   Muchos años   Is pollá éti

64

South Africa
arr. A. Nyberg

Seng' ya vuma/ Seng' ya vuma/ Seng' ya vuma Somandla.

Lead me Lord/ Lead me Jesus . . . lead me Lord.
Fill me.
I will go Lord,/ I will go Lord,. . . In your name, Lord, I will go.

Führe mich Herr/ Führ' mich Jesus. . . führ' mich Herr.
Fülle mich.

Guide-moi Seigneur/ Guide-moi Jésus. . .oui guide-moi.
Change-moi.

Guíame Dios. Guíame Dios. . . Llena-me de tu poder.
Yo iré, Dios. Yo iré, Dios. . . En tu nombre yo iré.

65   Sydney Carter: United Kingdom

2. Travel on, travel on there's a spirit that is growing,/ the spirit grows like flowers night and day./ Travel on, travel on with the flower that is growing,/ the spirit will be with us all the way.

3. Travel on, travel on there's a spirit that is playing,/ the spirit plays like music every day./ Travel on, travel on with the music that is playing,/ The spirit will be with us all the way.

4. In the kingdom of heav'n is our end and our beginning/ and the road that we must follow every day./ Travel on, travel on to the kingdom that is coming,/ the kingdom will be with us all the way.

The original first and third lines of verses 1,2 and 3 replaces the word "Spirit" with "River," "Flower" and "Music" respectively.

2. Geh den Weg, geh den Weg, denn du gehst ihn nicht alleine,/ der gute Geist wird stark and hilft dir viel./ Geh den Weg, geh den Weg, denn du gehst ihn nicht alleine,/ der gute Geist wird stark and hilft dir viel./ Geh den Weg, geh den Weg, denn du gehst ihn nicht alleine,/ ein guter Geist geht mit dir bis zum Ziel.

3. Geh den Weg, geh den Weg, denn du gehst ihn nicht alleine,/ ein guter Geist macht Mühsal dir zum Spiel./ Geh den Weg, geh den Weg, denn du gehst ihn nicht alleine,/ ein guter Geist macht Mühsal dir zum Spiel./ Geh den Weg, geh den Weg, denn du gehst ihn nicht alleine,/ ein guter Geist geht mit dir bis zum Ziel.

4. Unser Anfang und Ende liegen im Reich des Himmel,/ und wir gehen täglich Schritte auf es zu./ Geh den Weg, geh den Weg, bis zum Reich, das auf uns zukommt/ und bei uns bleiben wird für alle Zeit./ Geh den Weg, geh den Weg, bis zum Reich, das auf uns zukommt/ und bei uns bleiben wird für alle Zeit.

2. Voyageons, voyageons, l'Esprit nous environne./ L'Esprit fleurira le jour et la nuit. Voyageons, voyageons, l'Esprit nous environne./ L'Esprit nous conduira sur le chemin./ Voyageons, voyageons, l'Esprit nous environne./ L'Esprit nous conduira sur le chemin.

3. Voyageons, voyageons, l'Esprit nous interpelle./ L'Esprit chante en nous le jour et la nuit./ Voyageons, voyageons, l'Esprit nous interpelle./ L'Esprit nous conduira sur le chemin./ Voyageons, voyageons, l'Esprit nous interpelle,/ L'Esprit nous conduira sur le chemin.

4. Au royaume de Dieu tout commence et se termine,/ La route défil'le jour et la nuit./ Voyageons, voyageons, vers le royaume divin./ Le royaume à venir sur le chemin./ Voyageons, voyageons, vers le royaume divin,/ Le royaume à venir sur le chemin.

66

S.C. Molefe: South Africa

A - si - thi: A - men, si - ya - ku - du - mi - sa, A - si - thi:
Sing a - men: A - men, we praise your name O Lord, Sing a - men:
Singt a - men! A - men! Wir prei - sen Gott, den Herrn! Singt a - men!

A - men, si - ya - ku - du - mi - sa, A - si - thi: A - men, Ba - ba,
A - men, we praise your name O Lord, Sing a - men: A - men, a - men,
A - men! Wir prei - sen Gott, den Herrn! Singt A - men! A - men, a - men,

A - men, Ba - ba, A - men, si - ya - ku - du - mi - sa.
a - men, a - men, A - men, we praise your name O Lord.
a - men, a - men! A - men! Wir prei - sen Gott, den Herrn.

Sub-theme Index
Unterthemenverzeichnis
Index des Sous-thèmes
Indice de los Subtemas

Sub-theme 1: *Giver of life – Sustain your creation!*
Unterthema 1: *Spender des Lebens – Erhalt Deine Schöpfung!*
Sous-thème 1: *Esprit source de vie, garde ta création!*
Subtema 1: *Dador de vida – Mantén tu creación!*

Invocations / Anrufungen Invocations / Invocaciones	No. 9
Calls to worship / Aufruf zum Gottesdienst Invitations à la prière / Llamados a la adoración	No. 13
Praise and adoration / Lobpreis und Anbetung Louanges et adorations / Alabanzas y adoración	No. 18, 19, 20
Confessions / Bekenntnis Confessions des péchés / Confesiones	No. 25
Collects / Kollektengebete Recueillements / Recogimientos	No. 30
Intercessions / Fürbittgebete Intercessions / Intercesiones	No. 35, 39, 41, 44, 45, 47
Benedictions / Segen Bénédictions / Bendiciones	No. 45, 47, 55

Sub-theme 2: *Spirit of truth – Set us free!*
Unterthema 2: *Geist der Wahrheit – Mach uns frei!*
Sous-thème 2: *Esprit de vérité, libère-nous!*
Subtema 2: *Espíritu de verdad – Libéranos!*

Invocations / Anrufungen Invocations / Invocaciones	No. 3, 5, 7
Calls to worship / Aufruf zum Gottesdienst Invitations à la prière / Llamados a la adoración	No. 15
Confessions / Bekenntnis Confessions des péchés / Confesiones	No. 21, 27
Collects / Kollektengebete Recueillements / Recogimientos	No. 28, 29, 32

Intercessions / Fürbittgebete
Intercessions / Intercesiones   No. 37, 40, 43, 44, 48

Benedictions / Segen
Bénédictions / Bendiciones   No. 57

Sub-theme 3: *Spirit of Unity – Reconcile your people!*
Unterthema 3: *Geist der Einheit – Versöhne dein Volk!*
Sous-thème 3: *Esprit d'unité, réconcilie ton peuple!*
Subtema 3: *Espíritu de unidad – Reconcilia a tu pueblo!*

Invocations / Anrufungen
Invocations / Invocaciones   No. 1, 6, 8

Calls to worship / Aufruf zum Gottesdienst
Invitations à la prière / Llamados a la adoración   No. 11, 12

Confessions / Bekenntnis
Confessions des péchés / Confesiones   No. 22, 24

Collects / Kollektengebete
Recueillements / Colectas   No. 31

Intercessions / Fürbittgebete
Intercessions / Intercesiones   No. 35, 36, 38, 44, 49, 50

Benedictions / Segen
Bénédictions / Bendiciones   No. 52, 57

Sub-theme 4: *Holy Spirit – Transform and sanctify us!*
Unterthema 4: *Heiliger Geist – Verwandle und heilige uns!*
Sous-thème 4: *Esprit saint, transforme-nous et sanctifie-nous!*
Subtema 4: *Espíritu Santo – Transfórmanos y sanctifícanos!*

Invocations / Anrufungen
Invocations / Invocaciones   No. 2, 4, 5, 6

Calls to worship / Aufruf zum Gottesdienst
Invitations à la prière / Llamados a la adoración   No. 12, 14

Praise and adorations / Lobpreis und Anbetung
Louanges et adorations / Alabanzas y adoración   No. 17

Confessions / Bekenntnis
Confessions des péchés / Confesiones   No. 21, 23, 24, 26

Intercessions / Fürbittgebete
Intercessions / Intercesiones   No. 42, 44, 45, 46

Benedictions / Segen
Bénédictions / Benediciones   No. 51, 53, 56, 58

Sources
Quellenangaben
Sources
Fuentes

We wish to thank all those who have granted permission for the use of prayers, hymns and liturgical responses, and illustrations in this book. We have made every effort to trace and identify them correctly and to secure all the necessary permissions for reprinting. If we have erred in any way in the acknowledgments, or have unwittingly infringed any copyright, we apologize sincerely. We would be glad to make the necessary corrections in subsequent editions of this book.

Wir möchten uns bei allen bedanken, die uns den Abdruck der Gebete, Lieder, liturgischen Responsorien und Illustrationen in diesem Buch ermöglicht haben. Wir haben uns bemüht, die jeweiligen Referenzen so genau wie möglich festzustellen. Sollte uns in den Angaben ein Fehler unterlaufen sein oder sollten wir irrtümlicherweise ein Copyright verletzt haben, so bitten wir um Entschuldigung. Selbstverständlich werden wir alle Fehler in den nachfolgenden Auflagen korrigieren.

Nous tenons à remercier toutes les personnes qui nous ont autorisés à publier les prières, les cantiques et les répons liturgiques ainsi que les illustrations reproduites dans cet ouvrage. Nous avons fait tout notre possible pour retrouver leurs auteurs et obtenir les autorisations nécessaires à leur réimpression. Si toutefois nous avions fait une erreur dans l'attribution de ces œuvres, ou porté atteinte aux droits d'auteur de quiconque, nous nous en excusons très sincèrement et serons heureux d'apporter toute correction nécessaire dans les éditions ultérieures de notre livre.

Deseamos expresar nuestro agradecimiento a todas las personas que nos han autorizado a publicar las oraciones, los himnos y las respuestas litúrgicas así como las ilustraciones que figuran en este libro. Hemos hecho todo lo posible por identificarlas debidamente y por obtener los permisos necesarios de reimpresión. Si hubiera algún error en los datos, o cualquier desconocimiento involuntario de los derechos de autor, les pedimos disculpas. En ediciones posteriores de este libro nos será grato hacer las correcciones necesarias.

Prayers/Gebete/Prières/Oraciones

If there is no reference the source is unknown/Falls keine Referenz angegeben, Bezugsquelle unbekannt/S'il n'y a pas de référence, la source est inconnue/ Donde no se indica la referencia, se desconoce el origen.

1. in *Textes liturgiques:* Louons Dieu et célébrons la vie, © Masamba ma Mpolo et Mengi Kilandamoko, Zaïre, 1988.

2. Matin Hymn, Armenian Sunrise Office.

3. © Dorothy McMahon, Pitt Street Parish, Uniting Church in Australia, 244 Pitt Street, Sydney, N.S.W. 2000, Australia.

4. Invocation to the Holy Spirit, Orthodox Liturgy.

5. Eric Milner-White, © S.P.C.K., London, U.K. Used by permission.

7. "Litany of the Spirit", text © 1977, 1978, Michael Shaw and Paul Inwood, St. Thomas More Centre, London, U.K. Published in North America by OCP Publications. All rights reserved.

10. Coptic Orthodox Liturgy.

11. In *The Iona Community Worship Book*, © Iona Community/Wild Goose Publications, Pearce Institute, Govan, Glasgow, G51 3UT, Scotland. Used by permission.

13. © Dorothy McMahon, *op. cit.* No. 3.

14. © Iona Community/Wild Goose Publications, *op. cit.* No. 11.

16. Ancient Chinese, © Iona Community/Wild Goose Publications, *op. cit.* No. 11.

17. St. Anselm.

18. © Iona Community/Wild Goose Publications, *op. cit.* No. 11.

19. John L. Bell, © Iona Community/Wild Goose Publications, *op. cit.* No. 11.

20. © Central Board of Finance, Church of England.

21. Parts 1 and 2, John L. Bell, © Iona Community/Wild Goose Publications, *op. cit.* No. 11.

22. © Dorothy McMahon, *op. cit.* No. 3.

25. © Iona Community/Wild Goose Publications, *op. cit.* No. 11.

26. © 1990, Mercy Oduyoye.

28. In *All Desires Known*, © 1988, Janet Morley, Women in Theology and Movement for the Ordination of Women, Napier Hall, Hide Place, Vincent St., London SW1P 4NJ, U.K. Deutsch: *Preisen will ich Gott, meine Geliebte*, © Verlag Herder, Hermann-Herder-Strasse 4, Postfach, 7800 Feiburg im Breisgau, Germany.

29. © Janet Morley, *op. cit.* No. 28.

30. Samoa, © The Uniting Church in Australia Assembly Commission on Liturgy.

32. © Janet Morley, *op. cit.* No. 28.

35. © Mr. Sione Amanaki Havea, Methodist Church in Tonga, P.O.B. 51, Nuku'alofa, Tonga, South Pacific.

36. © Masamba ma Mpolo et Mengi Kilandamoko, *op. cit.* No. 1.

37. © Masamba ma Mpolo et Mengi Kilandamoko, *op. cit.* No. 1.

38. Armenian Orthodox Liturgy.

39. © Pitt Street Parish, *op. cit.* No. 3.

40. © Pitt Street Parish, *op. cit.* No. 3.

41. Evening Prayer of the Covenant, Ethiopian Orthodox Liturgy.

42. © Mamie Woungly-Massaga, Masamba ma Mpolo et Mengi Kilandamoko, *op. cit.* No. 1.

43. John L. Bell, © Iona Community/Wild Goose Publications, *op. cit.* No. 11.

44. © Dorothy McMahon, *op. cit.* No. 3.

45. Prayer for the Sick, Orthodox Liturgy.

46. The Divine Liturgy of St. Chrysostom, commemoration of the diptychs of the living.

47. © Iona Community/Wild Goose Publications, *op. cit.* No. 11.

49. Part 1 adapt. from the draft eucharistic liturgy, Church of the Province of Kenya. Parts 2 and 3 adapt. © Evangelical Lutheran Church in America, Chicago, IL, USA.

50. © 1990, Mercy Oduyoye.

51. © Iona Community/Wild Goose Publications, *op. cit.* No. 11.

52. Kiamu Cawidrone, Pacific.

54. © Bishop Vinton R. Anderson, St. Louis, MO, USA.

55. Adapt. Genesis 49:25-26.

Translation/Übersetzung/traduction/traducción:
English/Français: René Robert
Deutsch: Renate Sbeghen, Sabine Udodesku-Noll
Español: Noris Maldonado, Marta Palma, Ana Villanueva

Hymns and liturgical responses/Lieder und liturgische Responsorien/Cantiques et répons liturgiques/Himnos y responsorios litúrgicos

Adapt. = Adapted/Bearbeitet/Adaptation/Adaptado
Arr. = Arranged/Bearbeitet/Arrangement/Arreglado

M: Melody/Melodie/Mélodie/Melodia
O: Original
T: Text/Texte/Texto
d: German/deutsch/allemand/alemán
e: English/englisch/anglais/inglés
f: French/französisch/français/francés
s: Spanish/spanisch/espagnol/español

1. M: Notated by Dinah Reindorf, (d) Dieter Trautwein, (f) Joëlle Gouël, (s) Federico J. Pagura.

2. Music J. Berthier © Ateliers et Presses de Taizé, 71250 Taizé, France.

3. M: Russian Orthodox chant.

5. © with the kind permission of the Lutheran Theological College, Makumira, ELCT., P.O. Box 55, Usa River, Tanzania, (e) © 1990 Fred Kaan, (d) Gerhard Jasper.

6. © WCC Subunit on Renewal and Congregational Life and the Asian Institute for Liturgy and Music, notated by I-to Loh, (e) paraphrased by I-to Loh, (d) Wolfgang Leyk, (f) Joëlle Gouël.

7. © 1982 United Methodist Publishing House, 201 Eighth Ave., South, Nashville, TN, 37203 USA. Used by permission, (d) Dieter Trautwein, (s) Federico J. Pagura.

8. © WCC Subunit on Renewal and Congregational Life and the Asian Institute for Liturgy and Music, notated by I-to Loh, (e) paraphrased by I-to Loh, (d) Dieter Trautwein, (f) Joëlle Gouël.

9. © Evangelische Verlagsanstalt, G.m.b.H., Ziegelstrasse 30, Berlin, 1040 Germany.

10. © Asian Institute of Liturgy and Music, P.O. Box 3167, Manila 1099, Philippines, (e) © 1990 Fred Kaan, (d) Dieter Trautwein, (f) Joëlle Gouël.

11. © Pablo Sosa, Buenos Aires, Argentina, (d) Wolfgang Leyk, (f) Joëlle Gouël.

12. (d) Wolfgang Leyk, (f) Joëlle Gouël.

13. Greek Orthodox Chant, (f) Joëlle Gouël.

14. Music J. Berthier © Ateliers et Presses de Taizé, 71250 Taizé, France.

15. Greek Orthodox Chant.

16. © Dinah Reindorf.

17. © WCC, (f) Joëlle Gouël.

18. © Utryck, Box 3039, S-750 03 Uppsala, Sweden, (f) Joëlle Gouël.

19. Armenian Orthodox chant.

21. © Dinah Reindorf.

22. Russian Orthodox chant.

23. © Simei Monteiro.

24. © Christian Tamaela, Asian Institute of Liturgy and Music, P.O. Box 3167, Manila 1099, Philippines.

25. Arr. © 1975 CELEBRATION, P.O. Box 309, Aliquippa, PA 15001, USA, All rights reserved. Used by permission.

26. (d) Wolfgang Leyk, (f) Joëlle Gouël.

27. Used by permission M: © 1988, Iona Community/Wild Goose Publications, Pearce Institute, Govan, Glasgow, G51 3UT, Scotland, (d) Ingelina Nielsen, (f) Joëlle Gouël, (s) Federico J. Pagura.

28. © Guillermo Cuellar, (e) Linda McCrae, (d) adapt. Ingelina Nielsen, (f) Joëlle Gouël, adapt.

29. M: T:(O + e) © Per Harling, (d) Wolfgang Leyk, (f) Joëlle Gouël, (s) Raquel Achon.

30. © Asian Institute of Liturgy and Music, P.O. Box 3167, Manila 1099, Philippines, (d) Dieter Trautwein, (f) Joëlle Gouël, (s) Federico J. Pagura.

31. M: © Bertil Hallin, Sweden 1970, T: © Olov Hartman, Sweden 1970, (e) Maria Klasson Sundin, adapt. Per Harling, (f) Joëlle Gouël, (s) vs. 1-4 Pablo Sosa, vs. 5-9 Jorge Maldonado.

32. © Delbert Rice, (e) Delbert Rice adapt James Minchin © Asian Institute of Liturgy and Music, P.O. Box 3167, Manila 1099, Philippines.

33. T: © 1983 Nobuaki Hanaoka, arr. © 1983 Abingdon Press, 201 Eighth Ave., South, Nashville, TN, 37203 USA, (d) Dieter Trautwein, (f) Joëlle Gouël, (s) Pablo Sosa.

34. © Asian Institute of Liturgy and Music, P.O. Box 3167, Manila 1099, Philippines, (e) paraphrased by I-to Loh.

35. © 1982 "Señales y Cantos del Reino," Lois C. Kroehler, Apartado 2866, Cardenas, Cuba.

36. © "Ne Craignez Pas," G139, Texte: M. Scouarnec, Musique: J. Akepsimas. Studio SM, 3, Rue Nicolas Chuquet, 75017 Paris, France SM 260390-1, (e) © 1990 Fred Kaan.

37. © 1989 WCC, (e) Jaci Maraschin, (s) Jorge Rodríguez.

38. M: © Lynda Katsuno, T: © The Rev. Douglas L. Moschella Clark, (d) Wolfgang Leyk, (s) Rachel Achon.

39. T: © 1978, 1987 Medical Mission Sisters, 77 Sharman St., Hartford, CT 06105, USA, (d) Dieter Trautwein, (f) Joëlle Gouël.

40. Arr. Anders Nyberg, T: (O+e) Anders Nyberg and Jonas Jonson, © Utryck, Box 3039, S-750 03 Uppsala, Sweden, (f) Joëlle Gouël.

41. Used by permission T: © 1985, Iona Community/Wild Goose Publications, Pearce Institute, Govan, Glasgow, G51 3UT, Scotland, (f) Etienne de Peyer.

42. © Mrya Blyth 1989, (f) adapt. Hans Schmocker.

43. © Rev. Zoilo Yanapa, Centro Ecuménico de Promoción e Investigación de Teología Andina, Casilla 10221, La Paz, Bolivia.

44. © 1989 WCC, (e) Sonya Ingwersen, (s) Pablo Sosa.

45. All rights by © Dagmar Kamenzky, Musikverlag, Hamburg, Germany, (e) Irmgard Kindt-Siegwalt adapt., (s) Pablo Sosa.

46. Music J. Berthier © Ateliers et Presses de Taizé, 71250 Taizé, France.

47. © Per Harling, (e) Jonas Jonson adapt., (d) Wolfgang Leyk, (f) Joëlle Gouël.

48. © 1989 Lynda Katsuno, (d) Dieter Trautwein, (f) Joëlle Gouël, (s) Federico J. Pagura.

49. © Bishop Hassan Dehqani, Sohrab House, 1 Camberry Close, Basingstoke, Hants RG 21 3AG, U.K., Used by permission, (s) Pablo Sosa.

50. M: © Asian Institute of Liturgy and Music, P.O. Box 3167, Manila 1099, Philippines, T: © Shirley Murray, (d) Wolfgang Leyk, (f) Joëlle Gouël.

51. © 1985 Common Cup Company, 271 Queenston Street, Winnipeg, Manitoba, R3N OW9, Canada, (d) Sabine Udodesku-Noll, (f) Robert Faerber

52. Greek Orthodox Chant, (f) Joëlle Gouël.

53. M: © Suomen Evankelis-Luterilainen Kirkko, Virsien Julkaisuoikendet, PL 185, 00161 Helsinki 16, Finland, T: © by Anna-Maija Raittila on the basis of work by Pia Perkiö, (e) © Matti Kilpiö, (f) Joëlle Gouël.

54. © do Instituto Anglicano de Estudos Teológicos, Rua Borges Lagoa, 172-CEP 04038, Sao Paulo SP, Brasil, (e) Sonya Ingwersen © WCC (s) Jorge Rodríguez © WCC.

55. "Anna's Song," from *All Together Again*, by Robin Mann and Norm Habel, © Used by permission of Lutheran Publishing House, Adelaide, South Australia, Australia, (d) Wolfgang Leyk, (s) Pablo Sosa.

56. © Verlag Ernst Kaufmann, Lahr/Schwarzwald, Germany.

57 from *Sing Alleluia*, T: © Australian Hymn Book Co.

59. Music J. Berthier © Ateliers et Presses de Taizé, 71250 Taizé, France.

60. (d) Wolfgang Leyk, (f) Joëlle Gouël, (s) Federico J. Pagura.

61. © WCC Subunit on Renewal and Congregational Life and the Asian Institute for Liturgy and Music, (e) paraphrased by I-to Loh, (d) Dieter Trautwein, (f) Joëlle Gouël.

62. Arr. © Estate of Wendell Whalum. Used by permission. (d) Dieter Trautwein, (f) Joëlle Gouël.

64. © Utryck, Box 3039, S-750 03 Uppsala, Sweden, (f) Joëlle Gouël.

65. © Stainer & Bell Ltd., P.O. Box 110, 82 High Rd., London N2 9PW, U.K., (d) Wolfgang Leyk, (f) Joëlle Gouël.

66 From the *Lumko Song Book*, Arr. Dave Dargie, (e) Dave Dargie.

Illustrations/Illustrationen
Illustrations/Ilustraciones

1. Pentecost, by Sister Katharina Kraus, inspired by the Masai, Tanzania, Missie-Zendingskalendar 1989, Netherlands.

2. Pentecost, by W. Turun, Bali, 1962, gift from the Indonesian churches to the WCC.

3. Baptism of Christ by John the Baptist, red cedar panel by Tony Hunt, copyright Canadian Catholic Conference 1976. Reproduced with permission of the Canadian Conference of Catholic Bishops, Ottawa, Canada.

4. Icon of the Baptism of the Christ, photo by Nabil Selim Atalla, Church of St Mercurius, Cairo, Egypt.

5. Icon of Pentecost, Mount Athos, Greece, presently at St Paul's Church, Chambésy, Switzerland.

6. Spirit in action, Chile Committee Zurich (ed.): *Muralismo*, German/Spanish/English/French/Italian, ISBN 3 905482 58 4, Edition dia, St. Gallen/Berlin/Sao Paulo, 1990.

7. Worship in Spirit, Rarotonga, Cooks Islands, by Roland Feitknecht, Neuchâtel, Switzerland.

8. "A Mother's Love", by Maxime Noel — signs artwork with Sioux name IOYAN MANI, meaning "walk beyond". Copyright courtesy of Canadian Art Prints Inc., Publisher, Vancouver, Canada.